Praise for Daphne Rose Kingma

"Daphne Rose Kingma writes with such elegance that she could turn 'self-help' into a literary genre."

–L.A. Weekly

"Thought-provoking perspectives on relationships."

Praise for *The Ten Things to Do When Your Life Falls Apart*

"Anyone going through a dark night of the soul needs to have this book. It will be your closest companion and your most tender angel. Daphne Rose Kingma more than speaks to your soul; she knows how to heal it."

–Marianne Williamson, author of *A Return to Love*

Praise for *The Future of Love*

"In this innovative book, Daphne Rose Kingma breaks down the popular myth of how love is 'supposed' to be by introducing us to a broad spectrum of intimate connections. She reveals how to work through the various confrontations that every relationship encounters and reach deeper levels of love and intimacy."

—John Gray, author of
Men Are from Mars, Women Are from Venus

"Deeply insightful and daringly fresh, this book takes a breathtaking step away from tradition and into the possibility of saying yes to the true and grandest desire of our being: to love fully."

—Neale Donald Walsch, author of *Conversations with God*

Praise for *101 Ways to Have True Love in Your Life*

"Daphne Rose Kingma was my first teacher of the heart. With tender care, she taught me how to love myself and others. I can never express how grateful I am for all her wise advice about the profound practice of relationship."

—MJ Ryan, author of *Attitudes of Gratitude*

When You Think You're Not Enough

When You Think You're Not Enough

*The Four Life-Changing Steps
to Loving Yourself*

Daphne Rose Kingma

Conari Press

This edition first published in 2012 by Conari Press,
an imprint of Red Wheel/Weiser, LLC
With offices at:
665 Third Street, Suite 400
San Francisco, CA 94107
www.redwheelweiser.com

ISBN: 978-1-57324-534-0

Library of Congress Cataloging-in-Publication Data available upon request

Cover design by www.levanfisherdesign.com/BarbaraFisher

Printed in United States of America
QG
10 9 8 7 6 5 4 3 2 1

For you, because you've finally decided to love yourself
and because your soul knows you deserve no less

And in memory of my parents,
Jan Willem and Gezina Stuart Kingma,
who from so little
gave so much

Contents

Acknowledgments xi
Introduction xiii

_____Part One_____

Moving Forward, Looking Back *xvii*

ONE: Why You Need and
Deserve Your Own Love *1*

TWO: How Don't I Love Me?
Let Me Count the Ways *9*

THREE: How Did It Get to Be This Way? *31*

FOUR: Learning to Love Yourself *35*

_____Part Two_____

The Path to Self-Love *39*

FIVE: Speak Out *41*

SIX: Act Out *69*

SEVEN: Clear Out *95*

EIGHT: Set Out *125*

NINE: Living with Self-Compassion *143*

About the Author 155

Acknowledgments

L oving thanks and appreciation to Jan Johnson of Conari Press, who gave energy and inspiration to my vision for this book. Gratitude and heartfelt thanks to Mary Jane Ryan, for once again sharing her editorial gifts so generously with me. Thanks also to Don and Ana Li, who always welcome me home with open hearts and open arms. Much love and thanks to Molly, who moved our old oak dining room table into her new red dining room, so I could sit there and write with the Jack-dog at my feet. I.L.Y. Sweet love and thanks to Moe Bruce, Maureen McCarthy, and Zelle Nelson for sanctuary, love, and fun— and yes, for all those questions. Deep thanks and love to Rebecca Witjas for going to Bhutan with me, and also to Karma Gayley for the beauty of our trek. Special thanks to B.J. Hambleton for precious friendship, love, and sweet encouragement along the way; and a mystical rose bouquet of gratitude to Diane Dickerson. Your generosity in offering the sunlight of your soul and of your rooms allowed this book to be born in joy. If we could all love ourselves in the pure and gentle way you love all those who cross your path, Diane, this would be a world of exquisite sweetness. Thank you for your soul-deep hospitality.

Introduction

Unfortunately, in the years since I first offered this book, the issue of self-love has not become irrelevant. That's sad, of course, but in another way weirdly encouraging: the difficult feelings we all have from time to time about not being enough are, in fact, an invitation to each of us to develop a higher quality of self-regard.

Loving yourself is not an incidental undertaking. It's the most important job that each of us has come here to do. It's the one thing we really need to accomplish on behalf of the one and only person for whom we're totally responsible. It's also the key to opening the door to greater love, warmth, and intimacy in all our other relationships. Indeed, it's only when you reside in the nourishing feeling of loving yourself that you have a clear sense of what you seek in your relationships with others, as well as what you can offer them in return. When you know how good it feels to trust, honor, and enjoy yourself, you know that these same feelings, invested in someone else, can lift other people's spirits and give them a sense of their own value. In this way self-love becomes the standard not only for what we want to receive, but also for how to become a more loving person and have deeper, richer, and more meaningful relationships.

Self-love also serves another important function in our lives: it allows us to understand exactly what we have to offer to the world. As we come to recognize our specific gifts and talents, we also discover the specific purpose that we are here to accomplish.

The opposite of such life-enhancing self-regard is the haunting belief that you are somehow not enough. It generally shows up in the form of that creepy little dust-covered voice in the basement of your consciousness that keeps climbing up the stairs and telling you that you're not beautiful enough, tall enough, smart enough, educated enough, or intelligent enough to get chosen, to be loved, to succeed. You aren't a good enough parent, a sexy enough lover, a supportive enough spouse, a strong enough provider, a decisive enough leader, a submissive enough employee to get the outcome you desire. Even a chronic over-giving do-gooder type can worry about not *doing* enough: giving enough money, saying the right thing, bringing the right gift, choosing the best card. No matter what its specific message, one way or another the nasty little voice keeps wreaking havoc with your ongoing attempts to feel good about yourself.

Sometimes the voice makes a billboard pronouncement: "Of course he wasn't going to pick you, you idiot; you're not pretty enough." Or "How could you possibly make the right choice; you can't even decide what to order for dinner?" At other times, it seems to have taken up full-time residence on the couch of your consciousness and just plain laughs in your face when you try to make a concerted effort at loving yourself: "What's the point?" it says, "Good things never happen to you."

Why are we so darn hard on ourselves? Why are we always measuring ourselves against some invisible, perfect, utterly outrageous standard? Why can't we lay off? And if we *could* stop for even a minute—one friend told me she realized she hadn't beat herself up for four whole hours yesterday!—how can we replace the feeling of not-good-enoughness with the kind of positive, self-honoring self-celebration that could change not only us, but ultimately, everyone around us?

The good news is that you're not stuck with how you feel about yourself right now. There is a way to permanently change your self-concept, and this book offers a template for doing just that. We'll start by looking at the not entirely surprising origins of your self-deprecating opinions. Then you'll learn the four simple but profoundly life-changing steps to recognizing the beautiful truth of who you really are. Instead of continuing to rip yourself up with self-doubt, self-judgment, and second-guessing, you'll discover how to treat yourself with more acceptance, compassion, appreciation, and respect. Finally, you'll learn how to take this newly crafted sense of yourself and apply it to fulfilling the purpose that is uniquely yours in the world. Once you've done that, you'll find that the dance card of your life is so well filled that there just isn't any room for thinking that you're not enough.

If you'd like to come to peace with yourself, you might begin by answering these two simple questions: Who better to love you than you? What better undertaking could there be than to learn how to sweetly, happily, joyfully, generously, calmly, intelligently, compassionately, and respectfully love yourself?

Come. Take my hand. Let's take the first step.

Part One

Moving Forward, Looking Back

ONE

Why You Need and Deserve
Your Own Love

You, yourself, as much as anybody in the entire
universe, deserve your love and affection.

—Buddha

There is only one of you. You are a precious, unrepeat-able expression of the mind of God. It is confound-ingly simple to say that there will never be another you, but there won't. There is no one else who sees the world exactly like you do, whose feelings strike the strings of their heart exactly the same way as yours. There is no one, no matter how similar or familiar, whose days and years will be exactly like yours, no one else who can perfectly

1

nurture your dreams, who can most deeply feel each of your hopes as they fly like small butterflies into your heart or are crushed in the palm of a stranger.

Even if we all have thousands of lifetimes—and many people believe we do—the person you are in each of those lives is not *this* you, with this birth, these eyes and these hands and this pain to work out, these parents, these brothers and sisters, these talents, these gifts to give, this precise number of days and minutes and hours between the writing of your name on your birth certificate and its carving on your tombstone.

You're the only one who has the exceptional opportunity to truly know you and to discover your single beautiful path. Others can hold a mirror for you and show you parts of yourself that may have been obscured for a long time, but they can never give you the whole of yourself, the whole you that is yours to possess, to expend, to express, to release when your day in this life is through.

You can love others, care for them, encourage them, support them, listen to them, comfort them, joke and argue and cry with them—and I hope you do—but all the gifts of joy and consideration and nurturing that you give to others, you also deserve from yourself. You need the love that only you can give you.

Raw Beginnings, Deep Roots

Recently, at a party, I mentioned that I was writing a book on self-love. I saw a lot of heads turn. "Now, there's a topic," said the woman standing closest to me. "Self-love—I still struggle with self-hate. That's a deep black hole I've been trying to climb up out of for years."

There are thousands of reasons for not loving ourselves. Every person has one—or a hundred and one. We're too fat or too thin. We cry too easily, or not at all. We fear failure and success. We're foolish. We're not good enough, pretty enough, powerful enough, tall enough, brave enough, interesting enough. We convince ourselves we don't deserve the lives we desire.

Remember the proverb, "Love your neighbor as yourself"? Maybe we love our neighbors so poorly because we never learned how to love ourselves. Maybe we're trying to extract love from a love-starved self. Maybe, in order to repair our ability to love others, we need to start at square one—with ourselves.

In my own life, I always felt that I was superfluous and, in fact, a burden to my family. It wasn't because my parents didn't love me; indeed, they both showed me many beautiful expressions of love. It was because the circumstances of our life were difficult. I was the fifth child and fourth daughter in a family already struggling to make ends meet. While I was still very young, all my siblings became ill, two of them with life-threatening diseases, another with a protracted case of pneumonia. I remember watching my mother, weary beyond belief, single-handedly nurse all these ailing children. Day by day, I waited patiently on the stairs for the time when she would come to feed me. At those moments I felt sorry, apologetic almost, that after taking care of everyone and everything else, there was still another person—me—who needed her attention and care. Wouldn't things have been easier for everyone, my young subconscious asked, if only I hadn't been born?

Later this belief repeated itself when, as a young girl, I looked at my beautiful older sisters and concluded that, already, my family had enough girls. We were still having a very hard time financially, and it seemed that my being, my existence itself, was a burden to parents already stretched to the limit. I responded by trying to take up as little time, space, money, and care as possible. I practiced the art of being invisible. Trying to disappear is a long way from loving yourself.

My experience is only one of the multitudes of human experiences, many of them far more direct in their cruelty and impact, which make it difficult for us to love ourselves. We live through such experiences and come to adulthood, where we are expected to love others as ourselves but unfortunately, for many of us, the essential capacity to love ourselves is missing. This has profound implications not only for our capacity to feel happy and satisfied in our own lives, but also in our ability to love others.

When we haven't learned how to love ourselves well, we keep getting stuck on this simple first rung of the ladder. We don't know how or how well to treat others and we have problems with what we call boundaries. We stumble through the swamps of low self-esteem and thickets of self-loathing that derail us in our efforts to "love others as ourselves." It has been my own walk down the path to self-love that inspired me to write this book, as well as my witness of many others as they, too, took the journey.

In order to walk this path we must first understand that self-love is not narcissism. Nor is it egotism, greed, self-righteousness, self-involvement, stubbornness, or conceit, all of which have given real self-love a bad name. Rather, it is the singing spring from which each of us can become our most authentic self.

Self-love is also mysterious. For when we really learn to love ourselves, we no longer have to work at it every minute. By continually reminding ourselves how important we are, how important loving ourselves is, we eventually arrive at a place where self-compassion comes more easily, almost automatically. From the well of quiet acceptance, from the practice of a gentle unconditional care of ourselves, we can reach out to love others with exquisite generosity and bounteous open hearts.

That is because self-love is above all a spiritual matter. For it is only when we can actually see and feel ourselves as one of the threads in the vast human shawl, as deeply, indeed, unconditionally received by a passionately caring and beautifully ordered universe, that we can *truly* love ourselves. This true, felt sense of ourselves as a precious part of the universe is really the ultimate source from which we can love others.

While traveling in Italy recently, I met with a holistic physician who conducts workshops on self-care and spiritual practice. When I asked him what he found to be the most prevalent problem in his *medical* practice, he said, without an instant's hesitation, "People don't know how to love themselves."

Whether this rampant lack of self-love takes the form of physical affliction—obesity, addiction, and the myriad ailments which have at their source an unresolved emotional issue as in the doctor's practice—or whether it expresses itself as a so-called "psychological" problem—low self-esteem, relationship difficulties, problems with money—it's clear that there is an epidemic of our inability to love ourselves.

Indeed, I once heard a highly spiritually developed person say that it was easy to meditate six hours a day and it was easy to give away all his goods and serve his spiritual master; but when his teacher asked him if he loved himself he realized that he did not. In facing his answer to his teacher's question, he encountered the limits of his capacity to love.

It doesn't matter whether your own struggle to love yourself was born of difficult life circumstances or through some excruciating emotional or spiritual assaults—the wound is great. For so many of us, loving ourselves is our greatest emotional problem.

I have written many books about love: how to love well in a relationship, how to live through the end of one, how to inform your love and relationships with a spiritual dimension, how both women and men can learn to love and understand men better, how we can love people with personalities different from our own, and how all our loves are infused with that one great Love which is the light of being itself.

All of these instructions about love, however, are based on the notion that we already know how to love—to appreciate, apprehend, delight in, honor, value, esteem, praise, care for, empathize with, and even cherish—ourselves. If you're like me and a great many other people, you're probably still not an expert at this, your greatest life's work of love. And so I invite you to join me in this process of discovery.

This book is a journey to *you*, a discovery of how you lost yourself—and therefore lost your ability to love yourself. It is also a map to the beauty, the grace, and the strength that is you. It is *le beau chemin*, the beautiful route you will need to travel in order to reclaim them.

Loving yourself—truly receiving and cherishing your own being—is ultimately the task of a lifetime. Although the process can seem complex, at heart it's not very complicated. It's a matter of taking the four simple steps on the journey to loving yourself: speaking out, acting out, clearing out, and setting out. I describe these fours steps in part 2.

The brief stories I relate in the coming chapters illustrate by example the steps that others have taken on their path to self-compassion. They may not be precisely the steps that you need to take, but they can certainly point you in the right direction. I hope they will inspire you, and I encourage you to hold them up to yourself, take the parts that apply to you, and then use them to catapult you into action.

Change requires courage. Acting with courage, that is, behaving in ways that are unfamiliar and even scary to you, is what creates actual change. Once you have stepped—in thought, word, action or practice—across your own inner limits, you will actually start to function in new and different ways. This changed behavior will deeply affect the way you feel about yourself. Instead of discouragement or self-criticism, you will start to feel self-love.

With this in mind and with my encouragement and love, I urge you to take these four powerful steps on your own path to self-compassion.

May you enjoy the journey. And when you are finished, may your heart be full of *You*!

How Don't I Love Me?
Let Me Count the Ways

I can't believe how cruel I am to myself.
　　　—Woman, 36, recovering from a suicide attempt

D ifficulty loving ourselves is a universal problem. And far from being the best-kept secret of our individual selves, it's a creeping general malaise, something which, given a chance, we're all grateful to confess: "Oh, you have trouble loving yourself too; I thought I was the only one."

If it's true that so many of us struggle to love ourselves— if I nod with both recognition and shock when the Italian doctor states the problem, if the party people are cheering the fact that I'm speaking to this topic—how did it get to be this way? And why haven't we been able to do something about it? Why are we so seemingly uncomfortable in our own skins and why do we keep tripping ourselves up with so many kinds of self-sabotage?

Why are we sometimes able to notice this awful treatment of ourselves, but are still unable to prevent the next binge of self-criticism? And why, in our own private dialogues—those lying-awake-in-the-night conversations we sometimes have with ourselves—can we be so astonishingly brutal, not telling ourselves all the things that are right and good and beautiful about ourselves, but all that's wrong, bad, ugly, and hopeless about us? Why? Have we come to accept all this self-negating behavior as simply and unavoidably just the way things are?

One way to find the answer is to take a good look at all the ways we torture ourselves. Let's take a minute to drag the demons out into the light so you can stare them down before you move beyond them. I encourage you to look at this list without self-judgment. Just notice, with compassion if you can, how many of these things you do to yourself. Awareness is the beginning of healing.

Self-Criticism

My nose is too big, too small, too crooked, too pointy. My eyes are too dark, too light, too close together, too far apart. I'm too fat. I'm too thin. I'm too ugly. Why did I wear that fancy blouse—too dressy! Why did I wear that plain old sweatshirt—too shabby! I'm too wishy-washy, a patsy. I should have tried harder. I shouldn't have bothered. I shouldn't have said that.

I should've said *that* instead. I should've been nicer. More aggressive. Less blunt. I wasted way too much money on that hotel room, house, car. I didn't invest nearly enough money on that motel room, cottage, bicycle. I should've asked that cute girl out on a date. I was a fool to love him in the first place. It was the biggest mistake of my life to marry her. I should've been more patient with my mother. I should've gotten angry with my father. I should've blamed him more. I should've thanked him more. I should've forgiven him before he died.

Self-criticism is speaking badly about yourself and, in general, evaluating yourself in a negative manner. It is beating yourself up verbally for the sheer knee-jerk habit and indulgence of it, just because it's familiar to pick on yourself and put yourself down. Through self-criticism, you look at yourself and find yourself somehow unacceptable, not worthy of your own love.

Self-Blame

It's my fault my parents fought all the time—I wasn't a good daughter. It's my fault my child is sick—I didn't keep him away from that kid with the runny nose. It's my fault my husband is overweight—I don't cook him healthy meals. It's my fault my wife is unhappy—I don't earn enough money. It's my fault my favorite team didn't win—I didn't wear my rally cap. It's my fault that it snowed last night—I didn't pray to the sun gods. It'll be my fault if the house burns down—I don't check the electrical wiring weekly. It's my fault the economy crashed—I didn't manage my money well. It's my fault the ozone is depleted—I don't use the right hairspray.

A variation on self-criticism, self-blame is imagining—no, it's being absolutely sure—that, whatever's gone wrong, it's your fault. It's choosing to blame yourself rather than the ordinary changing vicissitudes of life or the people who are actually at fault, for whatever has gone awry. When your form of not loving yourself is self-blame, you tend to see every problem as somehow caused by you.

Self-Deprecation

I'm not valuable. I'm not special. I've no impact or meaning in the world. I really don't have any real talents. I don't write well enough, sing high enough, run fast enough. Okay, sure, I painted that picture, but it's awful, the composition's off, the colors are all wrong. I know how to tango, but what could be more meaningless? I'm lazy. So what, I'm raising three kids, working full-time, and taking care of my elderly mother—I could be doing a lot more. Let's not talk about my goodness and kindness—lots of people donate time at their church, buy armloads of Girl Scout cookies, let people in front of them in the grocery check-out line. And please, please, please don't tell me I have beautiful eyes, shiny hair, a bright soul—I don't, really. Just look at the television and magazines—I don't look like her! I could never wear that!

When you belittle yourself, you are not honoring yourself. Your talents, your actions, your hobbies—however ordinary they may seem to you—are actually your essence. They're all the extraordinary things you are; they're what you have to give. Denying your gifts is not honoring your spirit.

The media assaults us every day, all day, telling us that we're not good enough without buying their products, having a model body, or viewing the world their way. This information contaminates your precious brain, and if you're already not very good at loving yourself, it reinforces your sense of unworthiness. Surrendering to this media assault is a form of self-deprecation.

Self-Doubt

> Sure, I have years of experience, but there's got to be someone more qualified for the job. I'm not funny enough to go to open-mike night at the comedy club. I'm not quick enough to learn how to use a computer— if I tried, I'd break it for sure. I'm not smart enough to apply to law school—if I did, I'd probably be rejected. I can't confront my coworker—and, on second thought, maybe he didn't mean to steal my idea and present it to the boss.

If you suffer from self-doubt, you feel very unsure of yourself. Every time a challenge, obstacle, or opportunity arises, instead of taking a leap, you stand there frozen on your spot. Self-doubt blocks any effort toward change. And chances are your doubts aren't based on any empirical data; rather, you're just plain not loving yourself enough to risk the new and trust that your chances of success are as good or better than anyone else's. True, failure *is* one of the possible outcomes in any endeavor; but it's not the only outcome. Self-doubt is lack of self-love in action because it expects the negative outcome. It doesn't trust in joy, possibility, or a positive result for you.

Self-Deprivation

Even though it's a beautiful day, I think I'll stay inside and work. I get the popular brand of shampoo for my daughter, but the generic stuff is good enough for me. I'd love to have some of this wonderful perfume—on second thought, I think I'll surprise my sister with a gift. I'd like to get a new dress for the party, but why bother; I don't really need it. I'll have dessert but only if you want some too.

When you live with self-deprivation, you make an orphan out of yourself. You don't give yourself the treats and blessings of life. Everyone—even you—deserves to be delighted by the good things in life, big or small. Treating yourself as if you don't deserve the best, or maybe even anything, shortchanges you from the gift of yourself and from the gifts that others and life itself have in store for you.

Self-Destructiveness

I'm just committing suicide one cigarette at a time. I don't need to get my drinking under control. I'm almost finished—just one more hour at the computer, in the mall, in front of the television, at the office. I'm already fat, so what difference does it make if I eat another pint of ice cream? If I can just stretch this fast out one more day, I'll lose some more weight and then he'll like me.

There are many ways we can *physically* not love ourselves, ways we do unto ourselves things we would never consider doing unto others. When we are self-destructive we put ourselves in the very circumstances where the outcome is likely to be the exact opposite of what we need the most—health, happiness, confidence, fresh air, hope.

Self-Pity

Why does this *always* happen to me? Why does this *only* happen to me? God must be punishing me. I'm the only one who's ever felt this way. I'm so down that no one could possibly comfort me. I hope they don't even try. I'm a wreck. Why is my life always so hard?

Self-pity is dishonoring yourself, looking down on the grand, whole, becoming-at-every-moment-more-capable-self that you are. Pitying yourself is a condescending emotion. Rather than looking at the wounds and disappointments of your life as worthy of grieving over, as worthy of your own—and of others'—compassion, as being of value in shaping your life and your character; you wallow in a view of yourself as a small, inept, and pitiful human being.

Narcissism

Now that I've told you all about me, let's talk about you—what do you think of me? What do you think of my new haircut? I can't believe he cut it so short. This wedding is nice, but my wedding was fantastic. We had the best caterer; you should have seen the flowers. Why doesn't he call? I can't believe he hasn't called. We had

one of the best dates of my life. My daughter-in-law is
a terrible mother to my grandson. If I'd raised my son
like that she never would have married him.

Narcissism, to the untrained eye, can appear to be
self-love, but actually it's very hollow. It is immediately
tedious and ultimately exhausting to others. In fact, rather
than gaining the kind of loving attention that could make
you feel loved, narcissism engenders rejection and, in time,
the walking away of friends and strangers, leaving the nar-
cissist feeling abandoned rather than loved. Narcissism is
smoke, a lot of hot air and mirrors, false advertising that
leaves the real, beautiful person inside without a voice for
her wants, fears, needs, hopes, dreams, and aspirations.
Narcissism is a second-rate trip, a second-rate knock-off
of true self-love. It's produced, directed, and starred in by
the unreal self.

It All Boils Down to Low Self-Esteem

If you recognize yourself in one or more of the above
behaviors, you are probably suffering from low self-
esteem. What this means is that deep down inside, you feel
that you're not a very worthwhile person. Your opinion
of yourself never manages to rise up to the greatness level.
Monday through Sunday you don't think you're okay.
Instead of sparkling, you're always grey—a wannabe or a
has-been. You're not a player and you never will be.
You're not part of the in-crowd. You just don't believe in
yourself.

You may have your own additional, well-developed
ways of not loving yourself. Unfortunately, many of us are

world-class masters at the art. But whatever your method, each of these habits of low self-esteem is a symptom of something much deeper, something with roots in your childhood. And until you can look beneath the surface of your self-negating behaviors to see how you acquired them, it will be difficult for you to love yourself.

Whatever the form of your lack of self-love, you can begin to change it by understanding how you came to be so hard on yourself in the first place. Understanding is always the key to emotional healing.

THREE

How Did It Get to Be This Way?

Fear is that little darkroom where negatives are developed.

—Michael Pritchard

Children always follow their parents' example. We treat ourselves emotionally the way our parents treated us. If your parents treated you as if you were unworthy of their love—even if this was unintentional—you will feel unworthy of your own love. This will be true *until you consciously take steps to change the way you feel about yourself.*

We've heard a lot in recent years about "dysfunctional families," as if the majority of families actually *function,* as if it's only the rare or uniquely troubled family that's dysfunctional; but the truth is, every family is dysfunctional to some degree. Mine was. Yours is too. It isn't, in some ultimate sense, anyone's fault. It's in the nature of being human that our parents will have human failings. None of us has been loved perfectly, or even well enough. That's just the way it is. And that's why, as part of growing into our beauty as human beings, we must take up the task of learning to love ourselves. Ultimately, it's an inside job. It means going to the depths of yourself and getting acquainted with the lovely soul who deserves your support, care, affection, forgiveness, and compassion.

All issues of self-love are related to our sense of our own value, which is created very early on. When we're little, we depend on our parents to make life safe for us. When they fail to do so in some big or little way, our unconscious sense is that we aren't worthy of their love. We're not able to say that they're inept or inadequate parents, that they have human limitations. We can't say to ourselves that maybe they're still suffering from what they experienced with their own parents. Instead we say, *If they're not loving me the way I need to be loved, it must be my fault. I must be unlovable.* As children, we always interpret the lack of love we experience as somehow being our fault.

That's why the child who's left waiting on the stairs for food can't say to herself, *my parents are in a bind, they're overwhelmed by their circumstances.* Instead she says, *it would be better if I had never been born.* The child who's one of ten children feels like he's always in the way; the child of the busy brilliant professor grows up feeling she isn't smart enough; the son of the angry alcoholic father feels that his father wouldn't drink if only he behaved himself; the boy whose mother gave up her career as a fashion model feels guilty because being pregnant with him ruined her figure; the girl whose mother is deaf feels unworthy because her mother can't hear her; the teenager in the ghetto feels like a burden because her father disappeared.

Self-Worth and Fear of Death

In some sense, feelings of unworthiness are tied to our very sense of survival. Psychologically, it works like this: If I'm a good and perfect child, my parents will love me. If they love me, they'll take care of me. If they take care of me, I'll survive and thrive and become all that I'm meant to be. On the other hand, if I'm not good enough, they won't love me, they won't take care of me, and I won't survive. I'll be so neglected, I'll die.

This is not an entirely irrational fear. When we're young, we *are* completely dependent on our adult caregivers for our very survival. Somewhere inside we know this. Quite naturally, we feel that we'd better measure up ... or else.

In my case, for example, my infant fear was that because she was overwhelmed and overworked, my mother would forget to feed me, and I would starve to death. My friend Tom, the son of a raging alcoholic, was frequently beaten with any blunt object that was handy, and he legitimately felt that his life was in danger. And my friend Jane, who learned that her mother had tried to abort her, correctly sensed that at some point her mother had wished her dead.

Whether the danger is obvious, or merely implied, the bottom line of all this is that, psychologically, we believe we have to be lovable in order to survive. In this way, our sense of our own value is related to an unconscious fear of death. This is one of the reasons why, in adulthood, our own acts of not loving ourselves can feel so deeply violating. Each time we don't love ourselves, we are re-creating the unloved feeling we had as children. This make us feel once again as if our very lives are in danger. We're afraid we might treat ourselves so badly that we will die from the lack of our own self-love.

Your Life Theme

Everybody has a life theme, a significant psychological issue which they are working out in this life. Your life theme is created when a powerful emotional chord is struck in your childhood, and it is reinforced when similar events—events which carry the same emotional charge—reoccur throughout your life.

If, as an infant, you were left out screaming on the porch because your mother thought you'd grow up spoiled if you got attention every time you wanted it, you very likely experienced feelings of abandonment you couldn't put into words. It may have been years—many experiences or many relationships later—before you realized how deeply affected you were. But fast-forward a few years, when your boyfriend takes his third business trip in a month and then forgets your birthday and you "suddenly" feel like screaming because you feel so abandoned. When this happens, you are experiencing your life theme—abandonment—at work.

Your particular life theme may stem from the configuration of your family, the particular characteristics and limitations of your parents, the emotional dynamics between you and your siblings, or other circumstances of your life. But no matter what your theme, it will profoundly affect your sense of your own value and your capacity to love yourself.

Although each of us has our own personal variation, life themes fall into six broad categories, and generally, a single theme is most significant to your development. The major life themes are:

- Neglect
- Abandonment
- Abuse
- Rejection
- Emotional Suffocation
- Deprivation

Each of these themes has a powerful effect on how you feel about yourself. In childhood, as we have seen, it was the reason you thought you didn't deserve to be loved; in adulthood, it becomes the basis for your inability to love yourself.

Just as a life theme evolves over time, your sense of your own value is also incrementally created. Abuse by abuse, disappointment by disappointment, you create a self-concept based on your life theme and in time you will confirm your life theme by doing to yourself as an adult exactly the thing that was done to you as a child.

Your Life Theme and You: Cause and Effect

Perhaps you still haven't identified your own life theme. Or maybe it is so excruciatingly painful that you feel it's really all you know about yourself. Either way, it is intricately intertwined with the way you treat yourself now.

Whatever your particular scenario, it's important to become acquainted with it now. For when you identify your life theme, realize how it affected you in the past, and notice how you tend to perpetuate it in the present, you begin the healing process that will allow you to learn to love yourself.

Neglect

> Were you neglected, in terms of your physical, emotional, or spiritual care? Was your most significant relationship with the television set? Your best friend's parents? Drugs or alcohol? Was one of your parents an alcoholic? Did you live in a pig sty? Did your parents fail to teach you the basics of self-care, how to wash your face and brush your teeth and comb your hair?

If you were neglected, you tend to feel unworthy of the good things life has to offer and you tend to neglect yourself in the same way you were neglected early on. If you were left with the TV as a baby-sitter, never talked to by your parents, or not provided with the basic necessities, you probably don't know how to bring nourishing experiences into your life to sustain or inspire you. You neglect yourself.

You feel bad that you can't seem to buy the new coat, get yourself to the gym, stimulate your intelligence with good films or books, or find friends who will talk about the things that are important to you—and, most likely, you also beat yourself up for not giving yourself more or better attention.

Abandonment

Were you abandoned? Did one of your parents die? Was one of your parents away for a very long time during your childhood? Did one or both of your parents work so much that you hardly ever had any time to spend with them? Did your father disappear after your parents' divorce? Your mother? Were you emotionally abandoned? Did no one ever listen to or care about your feelings?

If you were abandoned, you tend to abandon yourself—that is, not stick up for yourself or be an ally to yourself in situations where you should clearly speak or act out on your own behalf. You probably also find yourself in situations where you are abandoned—your friends go off on a trip without you, you marry a workaholic who never comes home, your best friend moves across the country and then never writes or calls.

In general, you tend to be in relationships where people, for one reason or another, aren't able to be by your side or won't be loyal to you; and you very likely think that somehow this is your fault.

Abuse

Were you sexually or physically abused? Molested? Beaten? Were you verbally abused? Criticized, put down, made fun of? Were you emotionally abused? Were the nature, depth, and truth of your feelings ignored or denied? Were you called "too sensitive"? Were one or both of your parents narcissistic, that is, so impressed and involved with themselves that they took all the emotional attention, and gave none to you? Were you spiritually abused? In other words, do you have some special gift, intuition, or insight that was ignored or denigrated by your parents or siblings?

If you were abused emotionally, you tend to pick on yourself, be critical of yourself, put yourself down, and not feel that you deserve love, consideration, or care from others. You allow yourself to be treated poorly emotionally by others—let them run over your feelings, be hysterical in your presence, or critical of you; and you probably beat yourself up for allowing this to happen.

If you were physically or sexually abused you very likely perpetuate this abuse by not being kind to your body, not feeding it well, being overweight, having addictions that are physically destructive, or forming relationships with abusive people. You likely also blame yourself for not being able to find better situations and for once again allowing yourself to be treated so badly.

Rejection

Were you rejected? Did one of your parents wish you'd never been born? Did they wish you were a boy instead of a girl, or vice versa? Did you play second fiddle to another child in your family? A pack of siblings? A favored brother or sister? A twin? Were you in general ignored? Treated as if you didn't exist?

If you were rejected, you are likely to be self-rejecting, good at finding fault with yourself, and unconsciously seeking out experiences where you are not chosen or valued. You blame yourself for being in these situations but continue to find yourself drifting toward them anyway. Being left out and not being valued are familiar to you, and you tend to think this is all you deserve.

You very likely believe there's something about you which is the real reason you didn't get invited to the party—you're too loud or too shy—and why you aren't accepted by the group of friends you'd like to be a part of. You have difficulty feeling valued, feeling that you deserve to belong.

Emotional Suffocation

Were you emotionally suffocated? Did you have an overly protective or overly involved parent? Was one of your parents sexually seductive? Did one of your parents treat you as a spouse? Did one of your parents tell you all his or her troubles? Were your parents overbearing? Emotionally invasive? Did they insist on knowing your every move? Judging your every action? Did they forbid you to have any friends but them?

If you were emotionally suffocated or had to serve as a surrogate spouse to one of your parents, you often feel overwhelmed by people's simple desire for contact, and you are very likely commitment phobic. Because of this you feel frustrated in your desire for love, knowing you need and want it, but heading for the hills each time it shows up because of your fear of emotional suffocation.

You find some way to blame yourself for the fact that love eludes you and it can be difficult for you to take the normal, or, in your case, the very tender and gentle steps toward love that could resolve your life theme.

Deprivation

> Were you deprived? Did you grow up in poverty? Do
> without the basic necessities of life? Were you deprived
> of physical or emotional contact with one or both of
> your parents or siblings due to difficult circumstances?
> Did you grow up in a foster home? Were you emotion-
> ally deprived? Was your mother too busy or drunk or
> exhausted to give you any attention? Your father too
> busy reading the paper to ever talk to you?

If your life theme is deprivation, you tend to shortchange
yourself. You "do without," and feel that this is enough
for you, that you don't deserve more, or better, while at
the same time judging and criticizing yourself for not being
able to improve your situation.

You may keep to yourself, not allowing yourself to
receive from others, and then feel the reason you don't
is that somehow you don't deserve it. You feel that you
should provide better things for yourself while at the same
time blaming yourself for not doing just that.

You and Your Life Theme

Take a minute to think about what you've just read. Do
you understand your life theme now? Write down the
general theme that most accurately describes your history.
Then write about a few of the experiences that contributed
to the creation of your life theme. For example:

> My life theme is abandonment. I experienced it when
> my father left after my parents divorced and again
> when my mother died when I was twenty-three. I also
> experienced it when my dog, Toto, died and when Joe
> broke up with me.

My life theme is:

_____

_____

_____

_____

As you go along in this book and take steps to change the way you feel about yourself, notice how the behaviors that are most necessary for you to undertake on your own behalf are specifically related to your life theme.

Compensation and Your Theme

As we have seen, there are many events and experiences in your early childhood that combine to create your life theme. Your theme profoundly affects the way you feel about yourself. It also leads to the creation of a whole slew of behaviors you don't even realize you're developing. That's because one way or another, you start adjusting your behavior in response to your theme.

In psychological terms, this process is called compensation. Some children compensate for the fact that they're being treated imperfectly by trying to be better and better, by saying, in effect, I'll do everything my mother and father want—maybe that way they'll love me, maybe that way our life will improve. Now that Daddy's died, I'll take care of Mommy. If I'm really quiet, maybe Daddy will stop drinking. If I give them all my baby-sitting money, maybe we won't be so poor. If I do all the chores, maybe Mommy won't die of cancer. This is compensation in a positive direction. People who compensate in this way try to perfect their behavior in order to get loved, to resolve the painful issues that have contributed to their life theme.

But some children take another tack. They go along with the way they think their parents feel, and decide that their parents are right—they're not worth loving. In this kind of compensation, this child adopts a damaged and unloving view of himself. Instead of striving to gain parental approval, this child internalizes what he perceives to be his or her parents' view: They think I'm stupid, they're right, I'm not even going to try. That's right, there are too many children, I never should have been born. It's true, I'm not pretty, I'm a dog, I'll dye my hair green and mutilate my body. It's true, I do wreck everything they give me, I don't deserve a new bike. The problem with all this behavior, of course, is that it, too, is unloving. It often results in people giving up on themselves—acting out, becoming rebellious or self-destructive.

Whatever your form of adaptation, whether in a positive or a negative direction, instead of retaining the sense of yourself as whole and worthy of life and love, you have compensated for the fact that you were treated imperfectly. By trying to be better and better and better—or by giving up—you've learned very well how not to love yourself.

In this way your childhood, and especially your life theme, has set a pattern that can make it very difficult indeed for you to love yourself. But remarkably and wonderfully, this pattern can be changed. Let's see how.

FOUR

Learning to Love Yourself

The art of love ... is largely the art of
persistence.

—Albert Ellis

L oving yourself is the greatest work you will do in
this life. In a sense it is your only work. But as we
have already seen, the roots of your incapacity to love
yourself are deep. Indeed, you wouldn't have picked up
this book unless you felt you needed some help in learning to love yourself. Scientists tell us that habits make
deep inroads in the circuitry of our brains, that it takes
twenty-one days to start changing a habit and ninety
days to engrain that change. It's difficult to reverse these

complex brain patterns, and when it comes to redefining how we feel about ourselves, it can be especially difficult because many of these patterns have been encoded since infancy.

Because of the many ways we have learned how not to love ourselves, we have a good bit of work to do. We must learn to love ourselves in many places and many ways—in our relationships, in choosing our life's work, in doing our work, with our parents and children, among our friends and strangers, inside our own hearts, in the midst of all our see-sawy emotions, with respect to our bodies, and in how we choose to think about ourselves.

What It Means to Love Yourself

Imagine that everyone in the world is a hungry soul whose life has been imperfect. Like you, they had imperfect parents. Like you, tragedies and difficulties befell them. If you could hear each person's story, you would probably be moved to tears and want to reach out and embrace that person. You would want to tell them that in spite of everything they've gone through, they have great value.

You might also want to thank them for having the courage to move from where they came from to where they are now, expressing your admiration of their goodness and beauty and uniqueness. You would want to tell them that, indeed, certainly, in the eyes of God and also in your eyes, there's no question—they deserve to be loved.

Imagine that all these beautiful souls are standing before you, waiting for your blessing. When you look in your heart and ask yourself whether or not you can unabashedly give it, your heart spills over with generosity and laughter and love. You can't imagine anything easier or more natural than loving each person for exactly who he or she is.

Loving yourself means simply that you can imagine yourself at the head of the line of all these souls who are asking for your blessing, waiting for your approval. It means embracing yourself with the quiet heartfelt conviction of knowing that you're all right—that you're perfect—just as you are. Loving yourself is feeling, deeply, in your own heart, the quiet, steadying gift of your own intelligent love. Loving yourself means that, just as you're willing to rush to the aid of anyone else, you will rush to your own aid; you will come to your own rescue.

What to Expect at the End of the Journey

If loving yourself is the simple wholehearted acceptance of yourself, how will you know when you've arrived? Will you never again doubt yourself? Will everything be suddenly clear? Will you be a fat-headed egotist able to brag about yourself on a minute's notice and get whatever you want? Or is loving yourself something different? Day by day, week by week, year by year, what does it look like and feel like and act like?

Loving yourself is a quiet thing. You don't need blaring trumpets or a billboard to announce it to the world. Instead, when you've learned how to love yourself, you will feel the quiet inward turning of your consciousness toward you, to your value, to the unrepeatable beauty that you are. When you've learned to love yourself you will just quietly honor your body and mind, your heart, your emotions, and your precious eternal spirit. You will know that everything you are and all the steps on your journey have been purposeful, delivering you to the place where you can receive yourself with kindness and respect, forgiving all the missteps, honoring the lessons, growing in love for yourself and others. When you come to this peace you will have moved from the place of being a desperate, needy bag of tricks whose depression and self-loathing are like a black vortex that soaks up the energy from everyone around you, to being a person of wholeness, a person of joy and light who has something to contribute.

When you love yourself, you will also become more generous. You'll notice that it's not only you who gets loved, who receives the benefit. The whole world does. That's because each time you take a stand for your own value, the vessel of yourself becomes more filled with an abundance to share. Each time you move with grace another step down the path toward self-compassion, and arrive at a greater peace with yourself, you also hold the door open for others.

Through your uncompromised willingness to hold yourself in high regard, you will inspire others to do the same. Each time you affirm your own possibilities, you affirm the possibility that another human being will discover his or hers. Each time you decide not to beat yourself up, you create room for another person to celebrate herself. Each time you value—and then deliver—the gifts that are yours alone to share, you inspire others to give their gifts.

At its furthest reaches, your self-love becomes a gift of enlivening humanity, of creating the space where every person can finally come to the realization of his or her own divine being. In some profound sense, your love of yourself is a lifting up of the spirits of the downtrodden, a claiming of the high essence that resides in each of us whether or not we claim it. Each time you shine your light you become a reminder of the light that resides in each of us, each time you conquer your self-hate and self-doubt you radiate the spiritual essence that is the birthright of us all.

Just as negative attitudes have the power to circulate like a black cloud, so also will your sense of your own goodness be contagious. The more you can carefully and consciously honor who you are, the more others, basking in your example, will be able to honor who they are. Each person who claims his or her own value is holding the banner for all the rest of us. If you're not afraid to acknowledge your own value, then I won't have to be afraid to either. If you can strongly speak up for yourself, then I, too, can risk speaking out clearly on my own behalf. If you take the actions that honor and protect your body, your spirit, and your emotions, then I can also dare to take such actions. If you have the courage to clear out negative people, influences, and attitudes in your life, to rid yourself of unnecessary possessions and inappropriate attachments, then I can too. You are my North Star, my companion on the path. I can be inspired, can set my course by you. So it is that your own self-love generates to others. If you take the step; the world will follow you.

Your Gifts, Your Responsibility

As we have seen, one of the sad consequences of not loving ourselves is that we don't see the beauty and the uniqueness of who we are. We don't see our gifts; we don't think about what we're here on the planet to do. Instead of living inspired, fulfilled, contributing lives we're running around like crumpled balloons trying to gather enough oomph just to carry on. When you love yourself, however, you *can* give your gifts. It's that simple. And it's very important. Because the world needs your gifts.

Right now, you may not have a clear sense of what your gifts are, but once you start loving yourself, you will begin to get a sense of them. You'll also begin to ask the corollary questions of why you're here, and what you're supposed to be doing with your life. The more you love yourself, the more you'll begin to understand that you're not just here to feel great about yourself and your life, but you are also invited—indeed, required—to give your gifts, to use them. Giving and using your gifts will be part of your lifelong work of loving yourself.

What If You Don't Learn to Love Yourself?

Take a moment to consider the consequences of *not* learning to love yourself. Will an inability to love yourself:

- foil your attempts to pursue a life dream or chosen career?
- stand in the way of your taking good care of your body or acquiring a sense of physical well-being?
- prevent you from recognizing and utilizing some native gift of yours?
- affect your relationships—with colleagues, friends, your family?
- keep you from finding a relationship that could fulfill you, body and soul?

Given what you've discovered from the above, are you willing to take the steps to learn how to love yourself? In order to help you focus on your own process, consider the following:

What is the area in which you have the greatest difficulty in treating yourself well? Is it in taking care of your body? Eating well? Taking vitamins? Exercising? Maintaining a healthy weight? Getting enough rest? Addressing your body as the precious temple it is by treating it grandly from time to time with a manicure or a massage? Is it learning to shut down the inner judgmental voices? Is it about focusing and realizing your dreams? Standing up for yourself in relationships? Requiring the respect you deserve at work? Finding time for a spiritual practice? Giving yourself inner peace?

Then answer the following question:

- What are two specific results you'd like to get from learning to love yourself?

For example: Not hearing those nasty voices when I make a mistake. A feeling of self-confidence when I speak up. Not calling myself mean names. Feeling more confident when I go out on a date. Not getting embroiled with my brother's criticisms of me. Not criticizing my body every time I try on clothes. Feeling as if I'm successful enough. Daring to sing. Being able to tell Tom when I'm angry. Write the results in the space provided.

_____

_____

_____

_____

Moving through the Rest of This Book

The rest of the book is designed to teach you four specific steps—speaking out, acting out, clearing out, and setting out—to help you address your difficulties with loving yourself. How you apply them, though, will be unique to you, to what occurred in your life, and to your particular life theme. Read each section and make notes on how the teaching applies to you before going on to the next step. Or, if it is clear to you that you need to begin with one practice more than the others, start there, and then go on to the others later.

The examples I've used are offered in the hope that they will help you understand how to apply each step to yourself and also to help you see the connection between the problems you have with loving yourself and your life theme. If a particular story doesn't seem to apply precisely to you, look for the points of similarity anyway. See how it might shed some light on your own situation. Look for the deeper kindness toward yourself that you might learn from it.

I wish you well.

Part Two

The Path to
Self-Love

FIVE

Speak Out

Speak your mind, even if your voice shakes.

—Maggie Kuhn

Speaking is the language of the personality, the vibration of the soul. It is the energy of our essence formed into language, is the medium through which, as human beings, we reveal ourselves. Speech is power. It's how we make ourselves known—to ourselves, to one another, and to the world. It's the way we express the beautiful variations on the theme of being human that make us exactly and only who we are. It is the instrument of our interpersonal communication, the vehicle through which we tell others how to behave in order to treat us the way we would like and deserve to be treated.

That's why the first step on the path to loving yourself is to speak out. By speaking out, I mean expressing yourself in words. Taking the risk of saying the things you've never been able to say before. *Saying* what you need and want, what you hope for, what would make you happy. Saying what angers, disappoints, and irritates you. Saying what kind of support, passion, and friendship you need. Saying what you're scared of, what hurts, what feels wonderful, why this, that, or the other thing feels awful, why something else would feel a whole lot better.

Speaking out is different from just talking. When we talk, we simply communicate, put out information, share knowledge. But when you speak out there's a powerful charge to your speaking. Speaking out is more than reporting. It's you calling out from the depths of yourself to make yourself known, heard, and felt. You're speaking out on behalf of a cause. And that cause is yourself.

When you speak out, you affect the behavior of people whose actions have an impact on you, and you create the possibility for change. The changes that follow will be both internal and external. As you start presenting yourself in a new and self-affirming way, you gradually create the circumstances in which you are treated differently. You create a new beginning—not only in how you feel about yourself, but also in the way that other people interact with you. You'll start feel validated—and valuable—for who you are and what you have to say. You'll start really loving yourself.

Speaking Out and Your Silenced Self

One of the things to remember as you begin to speak out is that you're speaking out on behalf of your silenced self, the you who, until now, had no voice. If you'd always been able to say how you feel, ask for what you need, and express your hurt, discontent, and pain, you wouldn't need to learn how to do it now. And if all of the above were true—you wouldn't be reading this book—you'd be striding around the world with a grand and happy opinion of yourself.

As you gradually find the words to express your needs and feelings, you heal the part of you that was too afraid, too hurt or disregarded to ever dream of speaking up. This cowering silenced self gradually withers away and the you who cherishes you is born. You start to feel worthy of being loved—by yourself and everyone else—when you finally give words to your feelings.

Inside, we are a constant river of feelings. At any given moment, whether or not you're aware of it, you feel what's going on. You may not consciously know how you feel— now I'm happy, now I'm angry, now I'm irritated, now I'm feeling deprived or neglected or sad—but all these feelings are quietly recorded inside you. Taken all together, they form the way you feel about yourself.

Expressing your feelings gives value to who you are. Suppressing them makes you feel unworthy. When you speak out your feelings, they become the instruments by which you carve out a new and better opinion of yourself.

Speaking out is also the way you can best express your anger. By anger I don't mean gratuitous popping-your-cork anger; I mean the simple, direct expression of anger that arises when others treat you in a way that infringes on your well-being. Anger is important because it's the way you tell others how you want to be treated. It describes the consequences that will occur for them—you'll be angry, or you're angry now—if they don't treat you in ways that honor you.

Speaking Out and Your Childhood

When you speak out, you say *now* what you couldn't say *then*. In childhood, we all have many painful experiences that we can't talk about. Many of these occur long before we've acquired language. The infant left in wet blankets in his crib can't *say*, "Mommy, I'm cold, wet, and afraid. Please come get me and dry me off." The child relies on the parent to understand his need and respond to it. If that need isn't met, the child feels neglected.

The feeling of discomfort and abandonment gets filed inside, in the murky depths of your unconscious, and a whiff of the inability to love yourself is born. When more and more experiences like this are stacked up one on top of another, you start feeling unworthy. And if you were unable to speak about these disappointments the first several times they occurred—which is probably the case—you have by now developed the sense that whatever is bothering you is something you can't talk about.

The need to speak out doesn't arise only because there were things you suffered before you could speak. It also occurs if there were things you did speak up about when you were a child, but you were ignored or made fun of—either by simply not being heard, or by being deliberately disregarded, or by being criticized, judged, mocked, or put down. Maybe whenever you spoke up somebody said you were stupid, that you didn't know what you were talking about, your opinion was worthless, or nobody cared about what you were thinking

I know a man who, when he was a child, tried many times to tell his parents that their house was in danger of burning down. In school he'd learned about the danger of oily rags being stored too close to the furnace and repeatedly told his parents that they should attend to this fire hazard in their basement. But they never listened. In fact, his father told him that he had no business "telling them what to do." A few months later a serious fire destroyed two thirds of their house, but rather than acknowledging their son for the foresight of his warning, his parents bawled him out for "getting in the way" while they were trying to clean up after the fire.

The truth is that many childhood experiences affect us long before we can give voice to our feelings—either because we cannot or because we're too afraid. The child who is being sexually abused, for example, doesn't know if anybody will believe him, anyone will defend her. And the child who is being beaten by an alcoholic parent knows all too well that it's foolish to ask the abusing parent to stop.

We go through what we go through. If we're lucky, we're conscious enough to talk to ourselves about it. If we're not that lucky—if we're too young, or if it's too painful to mention it even to ourselves—we just experience it as a feeling which gets recorded in the cells of our body, only to be unraveled later, when we can finally speak out. When you speak out in the present, you give actual words to your feelings about the past. These feelings may have been hanging around inside you, unexpressed for years. If, as a child, your experiences brought you repeatedly into feelings of anger, disappointment, or frustration, this is the way you will come to feel about yourself. And it may be only because of a crisis in your adult life—an addiction, a shattering divorce, the loss of a job, the inability to discover your life's work—that you even begin to connect with these feelings.

When your lover leaves you, you may say to yourself, "I never could get his approval, just the way I could never get my father's approval." You finally make a connection. Or as you struggle with problem drinking, you may see that because the only way you could connect with your mother was to be her drinking buddy, you have inherited her addiction. Or as you wonder yet again what your life's work should be, you see that because your father never complimented your intelligence, you're still feeling so inadequate that you can't risk getting the education required for a meaningful job.

If, as a child, your experiences brought you repeatedly into feelings of anger, disappointment, or frustration, this is the way that, eventually, you will come to feel about yourself.

Being Heard

The truth can never be wrong—even if no one hears it.
—Mahatma Ghandi

One of the reasons we often don't speak out is that we feel hopeless about being heard. It's probably true that you haven't been heard in the past—by your parents, siblings, spouses, or friends—and so, in a sense, you have every reason to give up. There's a little crumpled-up part of you somewhere down inside that says, "Why bother? They never listened before, why would they listen now?" However, it's this very sense of defeat, this hopelessness, that created the feelings of unworthiness at the core of your inability to love yourself. Even though you weren't heard before, that's no reason not to express yourself now. Just because there's a chance—and in many cases a good chance—that you won't be heard yet again, don't give up before you begin.

We're so concerned about being heard because down in our silenced little psyches we believe that speaking up and getting heard are a pair of bookends, the alpha and the omega. We believe that it will only be worth all the anguish of speaking out if—and only if—we are heard. Even more specifically, we believe that we must be guaranteed the response we desire in order to risk speaking out.

This is the very assumption that caused you to keep your mouth shut all this time—guaranteeing that you didn't get any results, that you didn't feel any better about yourself. The truth is that it's worth it whenever you speak out on your own behalf, whether or not anyone hears or responds—*because you change your perception of yourself.*

Language creates reality. And when you speak out all the little pathways in your brain which, in the past, have been coursing with rivulets of self-criticism won't have such a big run-off of self-loathing running down them any longer. Whole new pathways will form in your brain, pathways where rivers of self-acceptance, cherishing, and understanding flow. Instead of dismissing your concerns as unimportant, you'll get a sense of your own value—simply because you've expressed it.

Even if nobody else is listening, you will hear it, the cosmos will hear it, and your battered psyche will hear it.

Speaking Out Changes the Voices in Your Head

When, as a child, you are subjected to repeated experiences of not having your needs met, it's almost as if there's a little voice inside that says, "Maybe I don't deserve to be cared for." Although you may not pay much attention to the little voice the first time you hear it, each time you are neglected, disappointed, or abused the little voice will keep repeating its message—until you finally believe that you really aren't deserving of love.

Instead of being able to speak out on your behalf, and say, "Things aren't right here, somebody should be taking better care of me," the little voice starts picking on you, saying you don't deserve the things you want and need. Instead of finding strength to speak out on your behalf, it, in effect, turns on you and says the reason you're not getting what you need is that you don't deserve it. Instead of defending you, or objectively observing the situation—your parents are too tired, too overworked, or too unconscious to give you what you need—the voice starts attacking you. It blames you for lacking what you need.

This attack voice is the voice of you not loving yourself. It is all the critical words, judgments, dismissals, and put-downs you've ever heard, taken inside, and then spoken back to you, by yourself. It's you, ganging up on yourself.

The attack voice is learned. It can be unlearned. The fact that at times it can get so loud that it seems like the only voice you can hear is all the more the reason you need so badly to find another voice, your real voice, the voice that will honor you.

The Ways of Speaking Out

There are three kinds of speaking out that you'll need to learn in order to take this step on your path to self-compassion. They are: Telling, Asking, and Expressing Anger.

Telling

As they were packing for their annual vacation to Hawaii, Paul told his wife Margaret that during their holiday, he intended to quit smoking. This was an extremely vulnerable thing for him to do since he'd tried to quit smoking several times before, and each time he'd failed, Margaret had openly ridiculed him. At a certain point in his failure process, he'd even join in with Margaret, saying he knew he'd never make it, that he'd been a fool even to try, and what could he possibly have been thinking?

Knowing all this, he was especially afraid this time even to mention that he'd packed nicotine patches and that he wanted more than anything else to break his addiction on this trip. As they were waiting at the airport, he finally had the nerve to tell Margaret. When she started to laugh in his face, he asked her to please be quiet and listen. He told her that this time he was serious, that he really needed her support. When she continued to laugh, he connected with some old anger.

As they sat waiting for the plane, he told her something he'd never revealed before: that she reminded him of his father. No matter what he had done, his father had always pooh-poohed him. Even when he'd graduated magna cum laude from the university, his father had put him down for not getting summa cum laude. For the whole of their marriage, Paul told her, Margaret had treated him in virtually the same way. Soon he was wiping tears from his eyes, and beside him Margaret was stunned. Finally he turned to her and said at point blank range: "So, are you going to support me or not, because if you're not, I'm going to take my bags and go home and you can go to Hawaii alone."

Margaret was surprised by his revelation. She had no idea that she'd been undermining his efforts. As for herself, she realized that Paul reminded her of her own father, a dreamer who'd always been scheming up schemes, none of which had ever worked out. It was true, she realized—she'd never thought that Paul could succeed. Taking a risk herself, Margaret told Paul all this. As she did, they both broke down and cried. Together they came to a deeper understanding of one another.

With Margaret's support and the nicotine patches, Paul was successful in quitting smoking by the end of their vacation. He hasn't smoked since. When he talks about how good he now feels about himself, Paul says he can't decide if the greater victory was quitting smoking or speaking up for himself. Margaret says the same thing, except she says that she feels better about herself because she risked saying the things that brought her and Paul closer together. Speaking out was a landmark for their relationship.

Telling is, quite simply, when we talk about ourselves. It's self-disclosure, revelation. It's showing, through the pictures of your words, just who you are. It's making yourself, with all your little and big imperfections, dreams and hopes, visible to the person or people you're speaking to. Telling means opening up your secrets and letting them see the clear light of day, risking that they (and you) will either be accepted or (your worst fear) rejected and made fun of. Telling is having the courage to reveal what's true about yourself, no matter what.

Telling may not sound like a big deal, but it is. It's a very big deal to express your fears and dreams. We all have secrets, things which for one reason or another we've kept carefully guarded. Sometimes we hide specific incidents in our lives, things we haven't dealt with or are ashamed of. Sometimes we hide facts and feelings about our parents. Sometimes we hide personal details about choices we've made or circumstances we've found ourselves in that we're embarrassed about. No matter what they are, when we hold our secrets in our unconscious, we can feel unlovable and unworthy because of them. In our psyches they can become the source of our shame.

Telling is revealing all the big and little things you feel uncomfortable about. It's revealing your scary truths and subtle sensitivities, and, in the light of your revelation, diminishing their power over you. Telling brings light to shame.

Some of the things we're afraid to reveal have to do with our circumstances. For example, Samantha found it very difficult to reveal the fact that when she was fourteen she was raped by her high school boyfriend. Ted was always afraid to proceed in relationships because in a terrible fire, which he himself had accidentally started, more than half of his body had been burned and now was covered with terrible scars. Luanne, a successful corporate executive, felt ashamed about telling that she'd been born and, until her adolescence, had lived with her family in a chicken coop. Jim didn't want his colleagues to know that, when his wife was ill, he'd had to declare bankruptcy.

Some of our secrets are about our parents: Sally was mortified to reveal that her father had been in prison for six years. Nat didn't want anybody to know that his father had lost his medical license for dispensing illegal drugs to high school students. Mark avoiding telling anyone that his mother was a manic-depressive, and Nancy, whose mother was a schizophrenic and would show up at school and start screaming at Nancy's teachers outside the schoolyard fence, preferred just to say that her mother was dead.

Some of these are about struggles and difficulties we've had on our own: Meg found it almost impossible to reveal that for years she'd been bulimic. Jack was ashamed that the only way he could lose weight was to have a gastric staple surgery. Julie, a fledgling attorney, didn't like anyone to know that because of her law school loans, she was still buying all her clothes at a second hand store.

When we reveal such things, our view of ourselves is no longer tainted by what we're withholding. Instead we see that the terrible (or vulnerable or beautiful) thing we felt too shy or ashamed to express is something that may be accepted by others—and even if it isn't, since we've had the courage to express it, it can finally be accepted by ourselves. Yes, I did live in a chicken coop; yes, I was raped; yes, I am scarred. By giving voice to our sorrows, we recognize that we are larger than them.

Asking

Sandra asked Ned, her boyfriend of five months, to communicate more consistently. She knew Ned cared for her, but sometimes he'd tell her he'd call "tomorrow" and then not call for several days. One day, after he'd promised he'd call her "tomorrow," but hadn't called for four days, Sandra decided to call him herself and tell him exactly how she felt. When she got ahold of him, she told him that while it was fine with her if he didn't call her for several days, it was not all right that he'd promise to call and then not keep his word. She asked him to keep his word from then on—if he said he would call, she told him she needed him to call. Then she went so far as to put him on notice, telling him that if this happened three more times, she'd break up with him.

Sandra once had a boyfriend whom she had virtually no way of reaching by phone. He couldn't be disturbed at work and he refused to get a cell phone. During their entire relationship, she'd felt either that he was cheating on her or that he didn't care enough about her to get a phone so they could communicate. After ten years of alternately nagging and beating herself up, Sandra finally broke up with him.

As she reviewed that situation and Ned's phone behavior, she realized that her father was a man with whom she could never connect. A busy lawyer, he often worked late. She'd sit around pining for him to come home and help her with her homework, as he had promised, but he'd often even forget to call to say that he couldn't make it. He'd come home so late that she'd already be asleep. Later she learned that he'd had a series of affairs, and that whenever her mother would call him at the office, his secretary would lie and say that he was at a deposition.

In Sandra's life, the phone represented the way that men disregarded women and proved that they were unworthy of love. As a child, she'd had no choice but to accept her father's behavior. With her previous boyfriend, she'd half-heartedly tried to speak out, but since she felt unworthy, as a consequence of her father's rejection, she never pressed the point. She'd left the relationship feeling her boyfriend had never really cared about her.

This time, when she finally asked Ned to change, he apologized. He said that in the business world he'd simply developed the habit of saying "talk to you tomorrow" as a sort of closure for his phone calls, and that he had no idea it affected Sandra so much. He promised that in the future he'd be more precise in communicating his intentions, because, it was true, he did care very much for her. There were two more occasions when Sandra had to speak to Ned about his casual phone behavior. Each time she did, she found it easier to speak out, and each time she felt much stronger and more self-assured in asking for what she needed. As the process continued, she also became more convinced of her own value.

For many people, asking is the most difficult form of speaking out. I once heard a man who was going through a devastating divorce say that the absolutely most difficult thing for him was to ask for anything at all. He said it wasn't manly. He said he'd rather drink himself under the table or work himself to death than ask for help, comfort, listening, or support. It defied, he said, his definition of himself as a man.

Not all of us feel quite so terrified of asking as this self-professed quintessentially *male* man, but for anyone with an issue of self-love, asking can be difficult. Asking—for the words, touches, reactions, gifts, responses, things to be done, ways to behave toward you, that you need—can be a very scary thing. That's because when we ask, we're vulnerable, and when we're vulnerable we're in touch with all the ways that we don't love ourselves. If you feel big, strong, handsome, whole, and worthy, it's not very scary to ask for the moon—or anything less. But if you feel small, unworthy, crinkled, and unsure of your own value, it can be very difficult indeed.

When you ask, you're revealing your lack, your need, a gap in the fabric of your reality. When you ask, you're taking the risk of asking another person to love and serve you in some particular way, and not because you're the king or the queen of the mountain, but because you're in need. Asking reveals your vulnerability. And whenever you reveal your vulnerability, you create a situation in which another person has power over you. You're in need; they can fulfill your need—and how they'll use their power remains to be seen. Will they lord it over you that you're the pitiful desperate unfulfilled person who needs their praise, help, support, and inspiration? Or will they lovingly, gladly give you what you've asked for because, unlike you, they have already seen your value—they love you, it is their joy to give to you.

Asking also opens you to another vulnerability. In revealing your need, you have to face any remaining questions of your "unworthiness." You have to step through the walls of your fears and behave as if you were already convinced enough of your own value to take a risk, to behave as if you're already deserving. Amazingly, you start feeling a little bit more as if you're as strong or worthy or deserving as you appeared to be because you had the courage to ask. Each time you ask, each time you do take the risk, the struggling-to-love-yourself you inside you is cheering you on and saying, "I knew you could do it! I knew you were worth it!" And each time you get results, you'll feel stronger, clearer, and more self-loving just because you did ask. Quietly, one step at a time, you'll be forming a fine new self-concept.

Expressing Anger

Sally went on a trip to New York with Karen, her best girlfriend. It was her first visit to New York and she was delighted by all the energy and excitement. One day when they were having lunch, an attractive man came in and sat at an adjoining table. Immediately captivated, Karen started flirting with him and, finally, invited him to join Sally and herself at their table. The minute he sat down with them, Karen started ignoring Sally, directing all her attention to the man, and not long after had secured a date with him. The three of them finished lunch, and afterward, rather than being in the mood to go shopping or even finish the conversation the two of them had been having, Karen was off in the clouds, talking on and on about the guy and where they were going on their date the next evening.

Sally was irritated but didn't know quite how to interrupt the flow of her friend's enthusiasm. However, when she checked in with herself, she saw that she felt angry about the whole strange turn of events. She'd been looking forward to the trip and now was feeling abandoned. Instead of having fun with Karen she was now playing second fiddle to her friend's budding romance. This felt a lot like when she was little and an only child. She'd be at home with her mother after school, eating cookies, talking, and watching television—but as soon as her father came home, her mother would suddenly get up, start mixing cocktails, turn all her attention on Sally's father, and treat Sally as if, suddenly, she didn't exist.

At first Sally descended into non-self-love, deciding that she didn't deserve any attention, that she must not be enough fun as a travel companion. But after thinking it over, she decided to take a risk. Sally confronted Karen and told her how angry she was about the way she was being treated. It wasn't acceptable, she said, for the two of them to go on a trip together and then have Karen virtually ignore her. She told Karen she was ready to leave and go home alone.

Karen realized the truth of what Sally had said. She apologized and asked Sally if there was anything she could do to make up for her distracted behavior. In the past, feeling she didn't deserve better, Sally would have passed it off as no big deal; but this time she said that either she'd like to go home and plan a different trip for the future, or that, despite her infatuation, she needed Karen to promise that the last two days of their trip would be spent with just the two of them sharing the pleasures of the city.

At the end, they did have two wonderful days together shopping and going to the theater. Karen repeatedly expressed how much she appreciated Sally's speaking out and how it had changed—for the better—Karen's opinion of her. Sally, too, felt better. By speaking out she had moved from the pit of not loving herself to affirming her own value. As they traveled home, both women agreed that the fact that Sally had expressed her anger had deepened their friendship.

Anger is a complicated emotion. It can go all the way from rip-roaring and utterly destructive rage to the firm and quiet expression of the fact that you are holding the emotional energy of anger about something that's been done to you. At its worst, and in our cliché understanding of anger, it's flying off the handle, blowing your stack, beating somebody up, being a raving, roaring maniac. These expressions of so-called anger represent the emotion of anger and the physical power of aggression combined. These are immature and inappropriate forms of anger, unleashed primarily for the benefit of the person who's unleashing them. At its worst, anger is the unbridled expression of these energies and this emotion. And that's why we're so afraid of it. Mostly, we don't know how to do it right.

However, anger is also a beautiful emotion. It's the emotion of self-care, of self-protection. It is the emotion by which we make ourselves known to others as worthy, valuable human beings. Anger is the way we tell other people that they've gone too far, that they've crossed the invisible boundary they shouldn't have crossed if they want to remain in our good graces. It's the sword by which we cut away behaviors that dishonor us, the emotion through which we teach others how to treat us well. Because there's always a strong and negative energy expressed with anger, people generally don't like it when other people are angry at them. There's a certain threat embodied in the energy of anger. There's the sense, when you're the recipient of it, that some negative effect could be unleashed in your direction. It is the presence of this potential threat which makes anger such a powerful emotion, and which also enables it to serve on behalf of our well-being. It takes a lot of energy to express anger; and it takes a lot of receptive strength and energy to be able to receive anger that has been delivered.

Speaking your anger doesn't mean becoming a raving hysterical maniac. It means determining exactly what you're angry about, expressing it strongly and clearly, and then elaborating, if you choose, about what it refers to in your larger life. By elaborating I mean explaining why it is that this particular behavior has the power to affect you so deeply. For example, "I'm angry that for the third time this week you're late. It makes me feel as if you don't care about me. It reminds me of how I used to sit waiting on the curb after school for my father, who would often make me wait for hours, and one time completely forgot to pick me up."

Elaborating is important because it gives the other person an opportunity to see you in the round, that is, to see and know you in the context of your entire life experience, and not just in the moment of your irritation with them. It gives them an opportunity to see what you've been through, and in so seeing, to love you better. And it gives you an opportunity to love yourself better because you see how the infraction of the moment is part of a long and knotted skein of infractions that have hurt your spirit over many years. You'll feel better because you will have honored yourself, and they'll feel better because they'll have regained your love and restored the harmony between you. Without self-indulgence or self-pity—other emotions that aren't really self-loving—you can look at yourself with a sweet compassionate eye as one who has suffered enough and now can—and must—speak out on your own behalf.

What Do You Need to Speak Out For?

Since in a great many ways we have all been silenced to one degree or another, it's often difficult even to contemplate what we need to speak out for. But there are many areas in which we need to express ourselves on our own behalf. Sometimes they're immediate things, and sometimes they have to do with a lifelong learning.

Patrick finally told Kathleen, his wife of eight years, that he just had to have a baby in order to feel fulfilled. Kathleen already had two children, ages nine and ten, from a previous marriage, and had clearly stated when she married Patrick that she'd already done her thing with children. At the time, Patrick agreed that her children would be enough to give him parental satisfaction, but as time went on, he realized more and more that for his own fulfillment he needed the experience of nurturing a young child, and that if he missed out on this experience, he would be so resentful that ultimately it could ruin their marriage.

After many back and forth discussions he finally had the courage to tell her that, although he was willing for her not to bear another child, he needed her to start the process of adoption within a year, and that if she couldn't, he might have to leave her. This wasn't a threat, he said, but rather the expression of a need that he could no longer ignore. Through his personal growth work he'd come to realize it was essential to his own sense of fulfillment that he be able to nurture a child.

Patrick was the sixth child and youngest son in a family of seven. He had two older brothers, and there were three sisters between him and his brothers. Both of his parents worked to support this busy family. When he was six, a baby girl, "an afterthought," had been born, and Patrick had become very attached to her, helping their mother with her care, feeding her, and even changing her diapers. When the baby was six months old, she died of unexplained crib death, leaving Patrick desolate, but also feeling guilty. Unconsciously he felt somehow that his connection to her was the reason for her death. He also missed her terribly.

When Patrick told Kathleen this story, and she saw how serious he was, her heart was touched. She agreed to begin the process of adoption immediately. A year and a half later their adorable baby girl arrived. Patrick was overjoyed and formed a special bond with his new daughter. Her arrival also strengthened the bond between him and Kathleen.

Whether your motivation is as deep as the desire for a child or as current as wanting to have more fun on your vacation, you'll learn to speak out by first paying attention to what you need.

To help you see what you might need to speak out for, answer the following questions. Focus on the two or three matters that seem most significant to you now—that is, the areas in which you are least satisfied with your life, and about which it seems most difficult to speak. On a piece of paper, write down both the following questions and your answers to them.

- How do you want to be loved and who do you need to talk to about it?
- What kind of affection do you want to receive and who do you need to tell about it?
- What kind of care do you need and who do you need to ask for it?
- What kind of comfort do you want and who do you need to speak to about it?
- What kind of protection do you require and who can you ask to give it to you?

- What do you need sexually and with whom do you need to share this?
- What kind of changes do you seek in yourself?
- What kind of changes do you seek from your partner and how can you ask her or him for them?
- What kind of changes do you seek in your workplace?
- What are your ambitions? What specific encouragement do you need about them? If you could think of one phrase to repeat to yourself in support of your ambitions, what would it be?
- What situation in your life has aroused your anger, caused you disappointment, or made you feel hurt? What would you need to say about this situation to bring yourself up to date with these feelings?

Keep the piece of paper in a place where you'll run into it frequently—inside the door of your medicine cabinet, in your lingerie drawer, above your tool bench. Make a point of speaking out about one or more of these items this week. If you like, you can also keep a record of each time you spoke up for yourself, and of the results you achieved— with the people you spoke to, and with yourself. As you answer these questions, you will come closer to knowing exactly what you have to say and to whom you need to say it.

Speaking Out Now

Whether it's expressing anger, making a request, or revealing something vulnerable, speaking out is one of the simplest and most difficult things you can do. To speak out you must first go inside and discover exactly what it is you need to say on your own behalf. Imagine exactly the words you need to say. Write them down if you have to. Sometimes a script can make speaking out a little easier when the time comes. This can be especially true if you'll be talking on the phone. You can look at your script, and feel supported by it, as you take the risk of communicating.

How will you know that you need to say something? You'll know when you contact an achy, gray, black, or even red feeling of discomfort somewhere inside you. Sometimes you'll feel it in your guts; sometimes it'll be an achy feeling behind your eyes. Sometimes it'll show up in your behavior (starting to hear the self-loathing voices, apologizing too much, overeating, reinstating a former bad habit). Or maybe in a passing situation, you'll hear the words you know you should say, but not have the nerve to say them. Sometimes you'll feel sick and think you're just sick, but find yourself wondering if maybe, by golly, there's something you need to get off your chest.

If you pay close attention you'll notice some of these physical indicators. That's because feelings are always expressed in the body. They can masquerade as an actual illness or just as feeling "sick" (as in, "I'm sick of the way Tom's treating me"). Sometimes they're subtle sensations, like aches, chills, or involuntary movements. At other times they can be violent physical reactions. For example, speaking to her friends about her anger at her father one night, Megan found herself suddenly having to run to the bathroom to throw up.

If you're having trouble figuring out what it is that you're feeling—and therefore, just what you might have to say—go to a therapist or an emotionally intelligent friend and ask them to help you discover just what you're feeling, and just how you might need to speak out.

When you need to speak out, your soul and your body will tell you. Your soul will tell you by sending you the message that the situation you are in is no longer acceptable to the highest level of your being. Your soul wants you to love yourself, to honor and cherish the single, precious and only you that you are. Your soul will use your body to help you to learn to love yourself.

When loving yourself takes the form of needing to speak out, you may hear the actual sounds of words circulating in your head. There may even be some editorial comments: "I really ought to tell Bob I'm angry at him; but I might lose my job." "I really want to ask Mark to take me on that vacation, but he might think I'm being too forward." "I ought to tell Todd I'm feeling sexually pressured, but if I do, he'll probably never ask me out on another date."

Or you may see your message, as if it were printed up like the letters in a little cartoon balloon or on a blackboard. But whatever the form in which your message is revealed to you, I hope you'll take it seriously. This is your deep self wanting you to risk loving yourself. The you who's learning to love yourself is showing or telling you that you need to speak out on your own behalf.

How to Speak Out

Sometimes life gives you a golden opportunity to speak out for yourself, but most of the time it doesn't. You may find a perfect opening in a conversation to say what you've always needed to say, or what you figured out yesterday you really should say to your mother or husband. There may be a deathbed moment when your father raises his head from a coma and asks if there's anything you need to say to him before he slips over into the next world. But chances are that most of the time, it won't be that easy. The circumstances for speaking out won't just fall into your lap; you'll have to create them.

For instance, you've been taking a class with a girl you've had a crush on for more than a year. She's just your type, you think; she's beautiful and kind and meets all the requirements of your personal laundry list for a potential mate. You're not sure exactly what her relationship status is, but you decide to find out. Pulling yourself up by your bootstraps, you make a pact with yourself that you'll tell her about your feelings on Friday, the 13th, come hell or high water. The day arrives, and although she's in a rush to go somewhere, you ask her to wait a few extra minutes, and you tell her about your feelings. She's taken aback, but politely drives off digesting what you've told her. Stay tuned—for an opportunity, or a possible rejection. In either case, you've honored yourself by speaking your mind—in this case, the mind of your heart.

There is a middle place between waiting for the right opportunity and making it happen, which is seizing the moment. For example, you've always had a difficult relationship with your father. In therapy you berated him, wrote him nasty, angry letters, gave him a piece of your mind. He was appalled, and reacted harshly, called you a railing hysterical bitch—what good had all that therapy done? Then he retreated for fourteen years. Now he's old, heading for death, the last five-star event of his life. You still haven't connected but have moved tentatively toward one another, sharing an occasional conversation or dinner. Instead of trying to drive it all home one more time—how hurt you are that he never called, never paid any attention—you simply look for an opportunity.

One night, you're having one of those mindless conversations you have with him over dinner, talking about the car you just bought and the price of gasoline. Searching for the words that will express how you really feel about your whole lifelong lack of connection, you finally say, "I'm sad that we never had more time, that we never really got to know each other." He's startled, looks up and across at you for a moment. His eyes grow glassy and teary as he looks right at you, the sorrow shiny in his eyes. He smiles a little sadly. For a nanosecond you have the connection you've always longed for.

When you know there's something you have to say, find the time to say it. The time may be now, the time may be soon, the time may be when you decide it is, or when there's an opportunity. Look for the time, or create it; but whatever you do, speak up. Then, notice how you feel after you've said what you needed to. Do you feel you love yourself more than you used to? Notice how your sense of your own value has improved.

Each time you speak out, you'll feel more deserving of what you are speaking out for. The more you do it, the easier it will become. Identify what you need to speak out for, and then do it. Speak out to reveal your hopes, fears, dreams, limitations, anger, intentions, heartaches, losses, embarrassments, ambitions. When you do, you will see how precious you are, how deserving of love. So start taking the risk. Speak out!

SIX

Act Out

Knowing is not enough; we must apply. Willing is not enough; we must do.

—Goethe

In psychological terms, acting out isn't ordinarily thought of as being a good thing. It usually means that instead of behaving like a conscious, forthright human being and talking about what you need, feel, or want, you "act out," that is, perform despicable behaviors like egging someone's car windshield or beating someone up in a dark alley. In this view, acting out is a kind of immature emotional behavior through which you indirectly express your feelings through action instead of simply stating them. In psychological terms, acting out is "passive-aggressive" behavior.

In the cliché marital transaction, for example, the woman who doesn't want to have sex and creates a headache to avoid it is acting out to create the outcome she desires. Rather than telling her husband she isn't interested, she feigns a headache and gets what she wants. The use of an action—in this case, getting sick—to communicate something you don't have the courage to communicate in words is what constitutes passive-aggressive behavior. It's called passive because it isn't direct, and aggressive because it actually constitutes a kind of emotional violation of the person against whom it's directed. Rather than acting out in a positive sense, it's a subtle emotional assault.

But now I'm asking you to act out as a way of loving yourself. In this case, rather than "acting out" in the negative psychological sense, I'm suggesting that you take action on your own behalf, that you act, instead of cogitate, contemplate, ponder, analyze, emote over, or dish to yourself or with friends about what you need, want, desire, and deserve. I'm suggesting that you move from thinking about what you might do, to actually doing it. That you move from talking about it—"I don't like the looks of my hair"—to doing it—getting a new haircut or dying your hair purple. The difference between these actions and what we usually think of as "acting out" is that these actions are conscious, are positive, and you do them on your own behalf.

There's a reason I'm using the term "acting out." I'm not just telling you to act—to take an action. I'm encouraging you to act *out*. It's the *out* part that's significant. When you act, you simply perform an action. You take a notion out of your head and do something about it. But when you act out, you take actions that are out of the usual frame of reference for your behavior. In other words, you do something different, something you've never done before, something you might have never imagined yourself doing.

When you act out, you put your feet and your hands where your mouth is. You put your money and your movement where your mouth is. You put your courage, creativity, imagination, and energy where your mouth is. Instead of hoping, whining, imagining, or complaining, you *do* something.

Action is thinking and speaking in motion. Action is change. Action is energy, a new beginning, the transformation of how things are into the way you'd like them to be. Acting out is important because when you take action your body feels the signature of that action in your cells and bones. Your body knows. Far inside it carries the memory of how you've always been responding to life and the world. Somewhere in all your cells there's an imprint of all the chances you've ever taken, and all the little constricted wrinkles that got formed because of your fear of taking action. When you take action, you will know, kinesthetically—that is, in the very physical substance of your being—that you have changed. The body that has bungee-jumped can never go back to the concept of itself it had before.

When I turned thirty, I made a decision that every year from then on, I'd do something I'd never done before—not just something new, but something distinctly challenging, perhaps even something that had a slight edge of fear attached to it. I noticed that the people who inspired me all lived with a sense of adventure, of daring, while the people who seemed to grow old in spirit were people who had nothing new in their lives, no growing edge. They tended to live in the past, "remembering when." I also noticed that there was a high correlation between people's self-esteem and the chances they'd taken on their own behalf.

I remember once casually asking my new eye doctor why he seemed so happy on that particular Monday morning, and he told me that he'd just been looking at some wonderful photographs of himself and his family. He told me that on a dare from his daughter, he'd packed himself and his wife and four children off to New Zealand for a whole year. They'd gotten back two weeks ago, but it had been a life-changing experience for all of them and he was still feeling great about himself for having done it. He then went on to explain that he'd been very sick as a child and had never played sports or ventured far from the little town where he grew up. He had come to think of himself as a coward and a very uninteresting person, but his self-esteem had skyrocketed when he successfully planned and carried out this dramatic family sabbatical.

After I made my decision, I started enacting my plan, and over the years "the thing I've never done before" has included such diverse things as studying yoga, learning the fox trot, trekking in the Himalayas, horseback riding, going to Venice, writing a book, changing my diet, quitting smoking, and falling in love. Each time I've set out on the venture of doing my new thing, it's been scary. I wasn't sure I'd like it. I wasn't sure I'd be good at it.

I wasn't sure I'd think it was worth all the time or money. But each time I tried something different I gained a part of myself—a sense of my strength, of my intuition, of my body's resilience, of my emotional courage, of my delight in life—even if the part of myself that I claimed was only my discernment, my right to say no to the same experience another time. The more I did, the better I felt about myself.

The Importance of Acting Out

As I discovered, doing new things gives you a sense of expansiveness, of aliveness, makes you feel that life is good, and that you can be a part of all that goodness. Both you and your world expand, become bigger than they were before. This kind of acting out gives you hope. You stop feeling trapped or limited by life, and you learn the healthy benefits of continuing to do something different from this initial step of expansiveness. Furthermore, in addition to the single action step you initially decide to take, you realize that every time you take a courageous new action, your sense of hope and your sense of your own goodness increases. Instead of feeling pinched and closed and small, you begin to feel worthy of the gifts of life. In short, you begin to love yourself more.

Acting out is important because, like speaking out, it creates results, but it brings those results to an even greater degree. When you act, you immediately get a sense that something has changed. No longer are you the desperate, depressed, unlovable, hopeless wimp you thought you were. You are the courageous, self-fulfilling person who can, by golly, go and get it—whatever it is—for yourself.

When you act, you can create a new reality for yourself—a reality that confirms and expresses your own value.

For instance, after being dumped by his last girlfriend, John felt completely worthless. A man in his mid-forties who'd already had one "unsuccessful" marriage, John had been devastated to find that his girlfriend, a woman whom he'd seriously considered marrying, had been cheating on him for months. He went into a terrible depression, feeling that this proved what his mother had always told him—that he'd always fail at relationships and nobody else could love him as much as she did.

John's father had walked out when he was a teenager and his mother, a scared, depressed, and psychologically dependent woman, became very possessive of John. Before he left, John's father had always criticized John for not being tough enough, and when John began to feel overwhelmed by all his mother's manipulations, he tried to get away from her by eloping with a girl he hardly knew. When this first marriage failed, his mother told him that he'd just proved it—only a mother could love him. Despite being riddled by all these negative past messages, John decided to take some dramatic action. He signed up for a singles workshop on building good relationships.

As the workshop progressed, he was so appreciated by all the other members of the workshop that when his birthday came around, they threw a surprise party for him. John was delighted. Through their warmhearted gesture, he saw that indeed, he was lovable, that even this group of relative strangers cared about him more than he'd ever imagined. Strengthened by the love he experienced with the group, John took a second initiative. When the workshop was over he called one of the participants and invited her out on a date. They dated for a year and now are joyfully married.

By stepping out and taking action despite his self-limiting beliefs, John found happiness.

Conscious Action

Whatever you can do or dream ... begin it now.

—Goethe

It's important to be conscious of the actions you take because, as we have seen, acting out can carry a negative charge, as with passive-aggressive behavior. Conscious action has profound effects. Because it is motivated by specific intention to achieve specific results, it will create a lot of movement in your world. Unlike an idea that's just swirling around in your head, conscious action is an idea unleashed and set into motion. Action has the ability to change the energy in your body, as well as in the people and things around you. Thinking about something is interesting; a thought can be the blueprint for what you want to do. But when you actually take the action you've imagined, you and your world begin to change.

Because action involves energy, the power inherent in the universe is mobilized the minute you take action. Each time you act, the energetic patterns of your life begin to change. The single action of the stone dropped in the pond creates not only the movement of the stone falling to the bottom, but also the ripples that shift the energetic body of the water. In a similar way, any action you take will achieve not only the specific desired results you intend, but also numerous other energetic responses in the world around you.

If you decide to get a divorce, for example, and then enact that decision, your action will accomplish not only what you intended—the conclusion of your relationship—it will also affect your children, your friends, and your colleagues at work. For example, Sarah told me that when she finally decided to end an emotionally abusive relationship with her husband, her mother was at first shocked but then began to take a look at her own life. Seeing her daughter's decision, Sarah's mother realized that she had never had the courage to end her own emotionally abusive relationship with Sarah's father. Inspired by her daughter's example, she finally found the strength to end her very difficult marriage of forty-two years. Because she had the strength to love herself by ending a destructive relationship, Sarah also provided the inspiration for her mother to do the same.

Acting out is powerful communication. It speaks for itself. The action you take will in itself reveal what it is that you need to affirm about yourself, or the new direction you need to take.

When I was a very little girl, my mother thought it was important for me to take afternoon naps. I didn't like naps. I recall feeling that spending an afternoon asleep was the waste of a beautiful day. One afternoon when I was once again lying down for a nap, I felt so bored that I decided to do something about it. I got up and tiptoed into my parents' bedroom and opened my mother's dresser drawer, where I knew she kept a beautiful box of white face powder. I wondered what it would look like sprinkled all over the floor like a dusting of snow. I took the powder and spilled it all over the floor. Then I stepped through it and watched with delight as the shape of my feet got imprinted in the white snow on the floor. Then, because that had been so much fun, I went on to find a pair of my mother's scissors to see what more fun I could have. Scissors in hand, I went back to my room where I started cutting out leaf and tree shaped patterns from the green wool blanket on top of my bed. Not long after, my mother heard me muffling around in my room, and came up to see what was going on. Rather than punishing me, she "got it" that I'd outgrown my need for a nap. In fact, from that day on, although we never discussed it, I never took another nap. Instead I whiled away my afternoons with crayons and scissors and paints beside my mother in her artist's studio.

I always like remembering this, because it's not only a story about me acting out; it's also about my mother's instant and beautiful recognition that I needed to express my creativity more than I needed another nap. To this day this remains true in my life—given a choice between resting and expressing myself, I'll always choose self-expression. My acting out had huge impact; at a very young age it set my life in a happy direction.

Acting Out and Your Childhood

One of the reasons it's often so difficult to take the actions we need to take on our own behalf is that, unlike in the story of me and my mother, when we were children our actions were often suppressed. We were told that certain actions were unacceptable. Out of their own fears, or out of a natural sense of protectiveness, your parents may have stifled your energy, your creativity, your passion (sexual or otherwise) your initiative, your strength: *Don't do that, you'll make a mess. Don't try that, you'll get hurt. Don't do that, what will the neighbors think? Don't wear that outfit, everybody will think you're weird.*

As part of the template of our upbringing, we're often told that certain actions are acceptable. As a consequence, rather than developing courage and originality in our behavior, our actions tend to become repetitive and unoriginal. In order to gain approval, to receive the love we think that we can't live without, we learn to draw our world of actions very small. Instead of being expansive adventurers, ever on the journey of discovering the expressions that will reveal us to ourselves (and in time become the vehicle by which we can also give ourselves to the world), we limit ourselves to the actions that we know will gain acceptance.

So it is that rather than wearing the chartreuse high heels and practicing singing in your bedroom, you learned to dress down and shut up. Or rather than becoming an actress, you became a secretary. Rather than taking a trip to India, you went to the mall. Rather than being a passionate lover, you lived in a passionless marriage for twenty-five years. One way or another, because of the content of your life theme, you learned to play safe, to contract, to limit your wholeness by living small, by living "according to the rules."

Given all this, it's hard to act out, and sometimes, rather than being inspired by expansiveness or a dream, the acting out that changes our lives is inspired by the constriction around us. This is true both when we do something our parents would never think of, or when our acting out takes a subdued direction because our parents made the world so unsafe and chaotic that, in reaction, we make our own worlds structured and calm.

Stephanie, whose socialite mother conducted numerous affairs in Stephanie's presence and right under her father's nose, acted out by not marrying the corporate lawyer of her mother's dreams, but rather a steady, good-hearted carpenter her mother would never approve of. When his parents insisted that Hank become a minister, he became a rock musician instead. When her mother said she'd better settle down and stay in her home town, Sharon, the star of her high school drama department, took off for New York. When Ken's father said Ken had to follow in his footsteps and become a doctor like he was, Ken got a job in cannery and later a Ph.D in religious studies. One way or another, the atmosphere our parents create around us defines the nature of our actions. We're afraid to act, we react, or we act in a different way because of the role that action played in our relationships with them.

When I was in college, I used to ride the bus every day for an hour on my way to my job at the hospital. Day after day I'd see the same older woman riding on my bus. As time went by we gradually had an opportunity to speak. One day when we were sitting next to each other, a person sitting across from us was reading a *Life* magazine with a photograph of some famous mountain climbers on its cover. The woman noticed the picture and remarked that it reminded her of her son. "When he was a teenager he just loved to climb mountains," she told me. Then she went on to tell me a lot of other unusual things he'd done when he was a boy and young man. I remarked that with all those experiences, he must be having a very interesting life. When I said that, the woman paused for a moment, and her face grew still. Then she told me that her son had died in a mountain climbing accident. I told her I was so sorry. When she turned to thank me, she said, "Well, that was his way; I wasn't surprised. He died being himself." Then she told me she'd always found peace with his death because he'd died doing something he loved.

Despite her own loss, this mother had a great enough heart to encompass that it was in her son's nature to climb mountains. She didn't stifle him; she even had the expansiveness of spirit to recognize that even in his death he was being exactly who he was meant to be.

What about Now?

The patterns of action or inaction that we develop in childhood are often so crystallized by the time we become adults that we're virtually unable to act on our own behalf. That is, we're only able to act in accordance with what we learned to do in relation to our parents. If they were wild and crazy, we've learned only how to pull in our reins and lead a life that seeks order and calm. Or, if they were constricted, shut down, and tense, we've learned only how to rebel, how to live on the wild side. It's only later—in a current life or relationship crisis—that we may discover the new kinds of actions we need to take to create some expansion for ourselves.

Whatever your repertoire of action in childhood, your current situation and present relationships will call you to a whole new array of actions. Vicki, for example, took such a dramtaic action that she amazed herself. She had been married for eight years to a man with a wandering eye. Not valuing herself enough, she tried to explain his behavior in a whole variety of ways: he was a photographer—it was understandable that he admired beauty; he was young when they married—he'd get over it; she was busy with the children—maybe she hadn't given him enough attention. Finally, remembering in therapy her endlessly self-indulgent mother, she decided in a single day to divorce him. She realized that tolerating his behavior was allowing herself to be treated in exactly the unloving way that she'd been treated as a child and that accepting his behavior was her current way of not loving herself.

Kinds of Acting Out

There are many areas in which you might need to act out. Here are some of the most common ones:

Taking Charge of Your Health

Kyle had been overweight for years. In his mid-thirties, he was more than 150 pounds overweight and was told by his physician that he was at serious risk for a heart attack. He felt terrible about himself. Although he'd tried many diets on and off, he could never stick to them. He'd lose ten or fifteen pounds, then start bingeing and, after his half-baked effort, end up even more overweight than before he'd begun.

Finally, he got so sick of all the diets his doctor had put him on, and the threat of having a gastric staple, that he went to a holistic healer. Under this person's guidance, Kyle went on a raw foods diet, started drinking veggie juice, and lost forty pounds. He started feeling so good under the new regime that a year and a half later, having lost all the weight he needed to, he adopted this new lifestyle permanently. He says that the way he now feels about himself is a hundred and eighty degrees different from how he used to. Creating a new body created self-esteem, he says. The simple—and of course not so simple—action of taking charge of his body was his path to loving himself.

Setting Limits with Others

LeeAnn's husband was a problem episodic drinker. One Saturday night, after yet another drinking binge, LeeAnn took all his things and threw them out on the porch in two huge plastic bags. When he came home drunk and punched a hole through the living room door, she went to the phone, called 911, and had him arrested. She had told him hundreds of times that his drinking was unacceptable, but, of course, he'd never heard her. That night she realized that just talking would never do it. Although several times before, she'd thought of taking action, on that particular Saturday night, she finally had the courage to do it.

After she did, she never let him back home. For a while he begged. He wheedled at all her weak places; but when she felt on the brink of giving in, she took another action—she started going to Al-Anon meetings. With the support of the people in Al Anon, she eventually took a third action. She divorced him.

Fulfilling Your Destiny

Tom had been the manager of a sporting goods store for years. The boss of sixteen employees, he was well paid and was always appreciated by those he managed. He was good at organization and he had "people skills." Tom loved history and had always wanted to be a college professor. He believed that history held great lessons for the present and was passionate about wanting to share those lessons with the next generation. He had stumbled into management as a young man, when, after his father's death at age forty-five, he'd had to pitch in and help support his younger brothers and sisters.

Now more than twenty years down the line, Tom was at his limit. He felt as if he had wasted his life. Fortunately, along the way, he had bought a couple of small houses as investment properties, one of which he lived in. One day, inspired by his misery, as he put it, he moved out of the house he was living in, took a room in someone else's house, and starting working part time so he could finish college. Finally he quit working altogether to get his master's degree. He is now a professor of history in a junior college, and working on his Ph.D. Teaching "fills his soul," he says. He's never felt better about himself than he does right now.

Being Who You Really Are
After feeling vaguely unhappy in her marriage for more than twenty years, Sue went to a career conference for women in hopes of developing a midlife career that would bring her a greater sense of satisfaction. Her son and daughter were grown, but she'd always felt that there was something wrong with her because, in spite of enjoying being a mother, she'd always felt so dissatisfied with herself.

While at the conference, Sue met a woman whom she found very inspiring. Lauren had created her own business and traveled around the country promoting the products she had developed. She was attractive and energetic, and obviously felt good about herself. One night after their sessions, Sue and Lauren went for a walk. As they walked across the conference campus, Lauren spontaneously put her arms around Sue and kissed her, and before she could censor herself, Sue responded by kissing Lauren passionately.

Amazed, even shocked by her behavior, Sue realized that Lauren had provided the missing link. Through that simple (and very complicated) transaction, Sue realized her true sexual identity. In a process that was long and at times very painful, Sue separated from her husband and began exploring relationships with women. She says that for the first time in her life, she now feels authentic—she's being who she really is—and that in spite of the sometimes difficult adjustments with her ex-husband and children she feels happier than she ever could have imagined.

Breaking through Fear
Dana went on a holiday camping trip to the mountains with her boyfriend, Grant, and his sister, Naomi. It was the first time she'd met Naomi and she was delighted that Grant wanted to introduce her to his sister. Once in the mountains, however, Dana started feeling bad. She was a city girl, and as Grant and Naomi plowed up the hills like two antelopes, Dana felt all the old feelings about being out of shape, not being athletic, and being clumsy and

incompetent in her body, the way her brother and the kids at school had always told her she was.

These feelings persisted when, an hour later, the three of them pitched camp under the mesquite trees up by the river. Grant was exhilarated to be there and at once noticed the old rope swing that dangled above the fast flowing river. "C'mon," he said to his sister. Naomi immediately scrambled up the rope, swung herself around, then let go and dived into the rushing river. A minute later, Grant followed, swinging the rope in huge circles, then letting go and diving in. Now along with feeling like a klutz, Dana was also feeling scared and abandoned.

Grant ran up out of the river, grabbed her hand and dragged her over to the rope swing. Dana was scared to death. She was starting to tell him there was no way she could ever do it, when an unexpected force took hold. She grabbed the rope, held tight to the giant knot at the bottom, swung herself out as far as she could, and then let go and dived in. She says that the minute she hit the water she felt reborn. To this day she cites the rope swing as the place where she found the courage to try anything. "My old scared klutz identity got washed away with the river," she says. Dana boosted her self-esteem in an instant, by grabbing hold of the rope and swinging through her fear.

Enhancing Your Sense of Your Own Value
After they'd been together six months, Bonnie bought her boyfriend a horse. She loved to ride and so did he, but he'd recently been laid off his job and was short of money. Bonnie owned her own horse and by renting another horse at the stables, Bonnie and Doug were able to go riding

together; this was one of their greatest pleasures. One day at the stables, they saw an announcement that one of the horses Doug had frequently ridden was for sale. The price was modest, and since she was doing well at work, Bonnie bought the horse for Doug.

Bonnie had been a very pretty little girl and her parents always told her she could get anything she wanted, just because of her looks. Although to some this might seem to be a compliment, the degree to which her parents emphasized how pretty she was made Bonnie feel that none of her other qualities had any value. In fact, she was constantly beating up on herself, because unlike other people whom she thought had real talents, or could use their brains, Bonnie thought that she was just another pretty face. Rather than giving her confidence, her parents' obsession with her looks made her feel that all she could do was sit around and be pretty and wait for someone to show up and take care of her for the rest of her life.

By the time she met Doug, she'd already taken the action of going to school and becoming a paralegal. When she had enough money, she bought herself a horse. Each of these things had made her feel more valuable, just in herself. But when she bought Doug his horse, she felt her own worth in a way she'd never felt before. She discovered herself as a person who could give and love. Although her parents ridiculed her—*you shouldn't be doing that for him; you're so pretty, he should be doing that for you!*—Bonnie found great strength in acting with generosity. In loving Doug, she also discovered a greater love for herself.

Living Where You Want to Live
Sonja had always hated the cold Connecticut winters and
dreamed of living in the sunshine. As a little girl she used
to draw pictures of palm trees on her school papers and
talk about the land of endless spring. Meanwhile, her
mother and father, themselves immigrants from Hungary,
told her she was a dreamer; they were lucky they were all
safe in America and she should just finish high school and
get a good job. Sonja did finish high school and get a good
job but she was unhappy. She felt hopeless and worthless
and trapped. The long winters depressed her.

One day she got a postcard from a high school friend
who was on a surf trip to Maui. Seeing the beautiful
beaches and waving palm trees, Sonja felt as if this was the
place she had always dreamed of. Excitedly, she told her
parents about Maui; they told her she was out of her mind.
But Sonja was hooked. She started working overtime,
saved all the money she could, and when she had enough,
bought a plane ticket, packed her bags, and without telling
her parents, took off. She has now lived in Maui six years,
and she loves it. Even her parents have come for a visit.
Although at times it's been a strain financially, Sonja has
never felt happier. Instead of living in self-denial, Sonja's
now living exactly where she wants to.

Expressing Your Grief
After feeling like a loser and never having a girlfriend in
high school, Hank started going steady his freshman year
in college. Four years later, he went off to graduate school,
expecting that when he finished his master's degree, he and
Sylvia would marry.

One weekend, when he went back home, Sylvia met him at the airport, announced she'd met another man, and told him this was the last time she would ever see him. Hank was devastated, returned to school, and became very depressed. He had all the cards and letters that Sylvia had ever sent him, and night after night would read them to himself, wishing and hoping that she would come back. Finally, he put the letters away and started dating again. He had some good times but, in the back of his mind, was always thinking of Sylvia and comparing every new girl to her.

Eventually Hank finished graduate school, got a job, and moved to another town. Although he made some good friends at work, he once again had a series of rather shallow, unsatisfying relationships. And once again he started beating himself up for being a loser, for being a guy who couldn't get a girl. When he finally did some deep personal work to explore this, he recounted that when he was a child his mother had loved him deeply, but then she had gotten cancer and died when he was eleven. His father, an unemotional man, had never allowed him to grieve, and within six months of Hank's mother's death, had married again.

One night after exploring his past, Hank went out to dinner with Paula, a female colleague from work. After Hank talked at length about Sylvia, Paula suggested they go to his house and look at the box of Sylvia's letters. While she was there, Paula encouraged Hank to read as many of them as he wanted to in her presence, and after he read them, suggested that if it felt right, he might eventually burn them all up in his fireplace. With Paula alternately sitting by and holding him, he wept uncontrollably as he read the letters one by one. Afterward he realized that along with grieving for the young man who had lost his first love, he was also grieving for the young boy who had lost his mother. He also realized that he was loving himself in the way that his father never had loved him—by finally allowing himself to grieve.

After expressing his grief, Hank said that he now felt very strong and clear. He said he felt as if could live without a girlfriend if he had to. But interestingly enough, a few weeks later he started dating Paula, the woman who had witnessed his outpouring of tears. Not long after that he mentioned that he had burned up all of Sylvia's letters and six months later he called to tell me that he and Paula were getting married.

How Do You Know When It's Time to Act Out?

The answer is simple: sometimes you'll know, and sometimes you won't. Sometimes you will thoughtfully take action, and sometimes you'll notice yourself spontaneously taking an action that will teach you what you want to change.

Any place in your life where you're stuck with not loving yourself can respond positively to the initiation of some action. For example, Julie was really frustrated with all the chaos and lack of focus in her life. She was in college, but she didn't seem to be able to apply herself. She wasn't getting good grades and she was beating herself up about all the money she'd spent to go to college and how little she was actually getting out of it. One day, visiting some friends in Arizona, she accompanied them to the Humane Society, where one of her friends was picking out a new kitten. While she was there, Julie walked past all the cages with puppies in them. One little black puppy stormed to the front of his cage and joyfully licked her hand. Without pausing for a moment, Julie decided to take the puppy home. In so doing, she acted on impulse—"a puppy's the last thing I needed," she says—and in a way that changed her life.

She'd been depressed and the puppy gave her joy. She'd been without structure and focus, and the puppy gave her structure and focus. When you see her romping happily with her dog, you can tell in an instant that Julie took the right action. She herself says that getting Canyon is the best thing she ever did for herself.

In other instances, unlike Julie, you may thoughtfully plan out an action. For example, you might decide that you'd feel better about yourself only by fulfilling your life dream, an undertaking that could constitute many steps of preparation, and then a concerted effort in taking those steps.

Because of family responsibilities, Bob had felt all his life that there was no way he could ever act on his dream, which was to sail from San Francisco to Mexico. But once his children were grown, he finally decided to do something about it. He started saving some money from every week's paycheck. A year later he bought a boat, and two years later he made the trip with some friends. He says that living his dream has totally changed the way he feels about himself. Instead of feeling like a loser who could never get anything he wanted, he says he now feels like a valuable person, a person worthy of his dreams. He says he now feels that anything else he could think of as being important to him is something he could also make happen, and that because of this, he thinks he'll die happy. Instead of feeling like a victim, Bob now feels in command of his life.

Your Turn

1. What would acting out consist of for you? What are the actions you could—or should—take right now on your own behalf? You might say, for example, that for you, acting out would consist of taking better care of your body: Going to bed early. Taking your vitamins every day. Exercising a couple of times every week. Throwing away all the cosmetics you know have toxic chemicals in them.

2. Write down the specific steps you would have to take to accomplish the full arc of action you have in mind. For example: calling the gym. Budgeting the money to join it. Buying a workout outfit. Checking out the route to the gym to see how long it would take you to get there. Figuring out how much earlier you'd have to get up in order to fit in a workout before you go to work.

3. What would be the consequences of taking this particular action in your life? In the way you feel about yourself? In the responses of others toward you?

In addition to taking new actions, stepping out of the familiar bounds of your own behavior, there are other ways of acting out on your own behalf. These are the action steps that you take in response to people, events, or situations in your world. In relation to your husband, for example, or your boss, your children, your lover, or the rude clerk at the department store. Because of what you experience with them, you take on a new behavior that will change the way you feel about yourself.

For example, Ellen, the mother of four, felt that she never had any time to herself, and she often whined about how hard her life was because of her husband and children. Finally, she got so sick of feeling so bad all the time that she decided to do something about it. She told her husband and children that every night after dinner, for forty-five minutes, she was going to take a time-out for herself. She used this time to meditate, take long healing baths, or sit quietly reading a book. At first her husband was incensed. How could she leave him alone with the kids for forty-five minutes every day? But Ellen held her ground. Without bitterness or complaining, she told her husband and kids that for the next forty-five minutes she was taking her time out.

Because she didn't do it nastily and because she was really just affirming her own value, Ellen was able not only to follow through with her plan, but also to change the way she felt about herself. In the process, she also changed the way her husband and children felt about her. Because she now felt relaxed and had taken some time to take care of herself, she stopped complaining. Because she stopped complaining, her husband appreciated her more. Because she felt renewed, the time she spent with her children was much sweeter. Now she was present when she was with them. She could really listen. After a while, instead of resenting the time she took for herself, her husband started protecting it for her. "Don't bother mom now; it's her time out," he'd say to the kids. Because he protected her time, she felt even closer to him. All in all, after six months, everybody agreed that Ellen's time out was the best thing she had ever done—not just for herself—but for everyone.

Similar self-affirming actions can be taken in all the contexts of your life—at work, with your siblings and friends, with people in social and business situations where you feel you're not being treated well. Instead of beating yourself up for buying the wrong car, you can stop taking it to the car dealership where they never seem to have the right part to repair it. Instead of blaming yourself for getting the wrong job because the people around your cubicle are always noisily gossiping about their boyfriends, you can buy a portable CD player, plug yourself in and listen to some wonderful music while you're working. If your best friend always makes you late for the movies by being late in arriving at your house, you can start going to her house to pick her up—or find a new friend with whom to go to the movies. If your sister always brings eggplant soufflé to the family Sunday night family potluck dinners, and you break out in hives because you're allergic to eggplant, you can stop eating it. And if your brother always tells you what a lousy tennis player you are, you can stop playing with him.

In every situation there's an opportunity either to act in your own behalf or to betray yourself. It's your choice. Of course, you won't always be able to take the self-loving action right off the bat. At first you may only be able to identify what that action might be. It might take three or four times of being subjected to a particular person or situation before you can screw up your courage enough to actually take action. But even thinking about the problem in a new self-loving way is an action. It starts the ball rolling. And each time you follow it through with new behavior, you'll start feeling better—because you have honored yourself.

Taking action creates change. You don't even have to feel really good about yourself in order to take the action; *taking the action will make you feel good about yourself.* It's magic. When you go to the gym and create a stronger body, you will feel better about yourself. When you paint your bedroom pink, you will feel happier. When you sign up for the piano lessons you've always wanted to take, you will feel joyful. When you act as if you're worthy of the changes you desire, you will start feeling worthy of them. Taking action re-shapes your consciousness. Taking action will help you discover your love for yourself.

SEVEN

Clear Out

In emptiness there is room for so much.

—Albertus Bratt

To clear out means both to remove and to make room for. In terms of loving yourself, clearing out is making a space of clarity for yourself. This is the third and very important step on the path to loving yourself. When you clear out, you create a clearing—in your psyche, in your environment, in your brain, in your house, on your dance card, in your closet, on your kitchen table, in the clutter of your conscious mind, and in the dark rooms of your unconscious where you hold yourself in bad opinion. The term clearing itself is a very beautiful word. When you think of a clearing in nature, you think of a clearing in the forest, a beautiful space in which sunlight can fall, in which new things can grow.

A number of years ago when I was traveling in Germany, I had the pleasure of driving mile after mile through soft rolling hills that were covered with tight-knit forests of tall, black trees. From time to time there would be a clearing in the forest, an open expanse of land where tree by tree the land had been cleared so that a village could be built or a beautiful vegetable garden planted. As I saw these gentle spaces in the midst of the forests, I contemplated the magnitude of energy, the many hours of sheer manpower, the number of saws and axes and horses and wagons required to make peace and space in the middle of these dense forests, the labor of love by which a clearing had been made.

On your own path to self-love, it will be both good and necessary to make a clearing in the darkness of your inability to love yourself. Like the beautiful openness in the forests I traveled through, making a clearing is not an easy task. It requires energy and steadfastness and strength. It will require courage and intention. To clear out from your life what doesn't belong will require devotion, not only to the task, to the labor of clearing out, but also—and above all—to yourself.

The Value of Being Clear

When we are clear, the world is clear to us. When we have clarity of mind and heart, we know what to choose, where to go, and whom to travel with. When your body is clear— of chemical toxins, negative emotional residue, excess weight, and mental chatter—your soul can proceed in the

When You Think You're Not Enough

direction of goodness, truth, and beauty. When your body and mind and heart are all clear, you can move steadfastly in the direction of loving yourself.

When your life is cluttered in any way, on the other hand, it's hard to have this clarity. When your garage is crammed with old paint cans and rags, broken down bicycles and last year's plastic Christmas tree it's hard to see where to park the car without bumping into something. When your mind is cluttered with self-judgment and accusation, it's hard to see your talents. When your heart is clumped up by self-doubt, it's hard to find love. When your body is compromised by a lack of self-care, it's hard to be clear about your destiny.

When your body, your mind, your heart, or your spiritual being is cluttered with what doesn't belong there, it's hard to see who you are. It's hard to become what your highest self is asking you to be, and it's almost impossible to love yourself. Because clutter and complexity are opposites of clarity—the accurate self-seeing that is love—it is of the utmost importance that you clear things out.

Seeing your self accurately and accepting what you see ... is love.

One process for attaining clarity used by the Quakers is called the clearness committee. In it a person convenes a group of at least four people to ask him or her questions on an issue about which he or she wants clarity. The person might ask, for example, why do I end up taking care of others? Or, why is it that it's so difficult for me to get out of debt? Each of these people then asks the questioner a series of open-ended questions, that is, questions which contain neither judgment, nor any of the questioner's own prejudice as to what the answer should be. As these "open-ended questions" are asked, and the person speaks out his answers to each one of them, he gradually gains clarity about the matter that was unclear in his mind. By approaching his own question through new and unfamiliar avenues, the questioner is able to approach his issue in a very different way, cleared of his own pre-judgments and habitual responses. Thus, a clearing is created in his mind. This process, itself a gift of love, was given to me by two dear friends on a recent birthday and set the stage with clarity for my own coming new year.

You can find clarity for yourself by doing the following simple process. On a clean piece of paper, pose a question about which you seek clarity in your life. For example, you might ask "What is standing between me and finding my true love?" Or "Why is it so difficult for me to find my life's work?"

Then, very quickly, without thinking, write the first five answers that come to mind, no matter how ridiculous they might seem. Put the paper away and don't think about it for a while.

The next day or several days later, ask five people you know to respond to the question you have posed to yourself. "Rob, why do *you* think it's so hard for me to fall in love?" "Jan, why do *you* think I don't have a boyfriend?" Collect the answers and write them down on a second piece of paper. When you've heard from everyone you have queried, compare your own off-the-cuff, instinctual answers with theirs. You'll be surprised at how they intersect. Somewhere inside yourself, you're already clear about the question you think is still baffling you, and you'll be amazed to see that your friends' and strangers' opinions will remarkably converge with some of your own points.

Eric asked himself why he had so much trouble getting a "real" job. His five answers were, "I'm not educated enough." "I'm scared." "My past was too hard." "I don't have the right clothes." "I'd be shocked if I succeeded." Over the next week, he asked five people the same question. Paul, his best friend, said "You'd have to get over thinking you aren't smart." Eric's little sister said "You'd have to forgive Mom and Dad." His brother said "You'd be amazed by your success." A girl at the lunch counter said "I have no idea." And the person who worked with him at the computer store said "You're very smart, but you don't seem to believe it."

Taken together, these reponses from others correlated very highly with Eric's own ideas that he wasn't smart enough and that he might be afraid of success.

Whether or not you are gifted with an opportunity to acquire clarity of consciousness from a clearness committee or you gain it on your own, attaining it is of the greatest importance. When your issue is loving yourself, this clearing provides the space for you to move from an old to a new way of viewing yourself, from a negative to a positive self-concept.

Clearing and Your Self-Concept

We all have some basic idea of who we are, what's good and bad about us, what we're total failures at, and what we've got a fairly good chance of achieving. Psychologists call this notion—and we all have one—our "self-concept." In a person who loves him- or herself, this notion of who they are matches up pretty well with who they actually are and how other people see them. In people who have difficulty loving themselves, on the other hand, this picture is significantly distorted due to the mental habits described in chapter 2.

People who have difficulty loving themselves have a "poor self-concept." That is, they have one or several opinions about themselves which are inaccurate in a negative direction, and which, in spite of their desire to feel better about themselves, they unconsciously perpetuate. Even if you know you'd like to love yourself better, you may tell yourself many times a day, in a variety of ways, that you aren't good enough. The ways you communicate this may be spoken or internal statements you make about yourself. Or your poor self-concept may be demonstrated through such self-dishonoring behaviors as overeating, addictions, excessive television watching, or obsessive Internet surfing. With an incorrect self-concept, a person will say such things as "I can't do anything right, I'm hopeless, I'm fat" (when they're actually twenty pounds underweight) or "Nobody'll ever fall in love with me," when, in fact, they've already had a number of successful relationships.

The good news about your self-concept is that, even if you have a bad one, you can change it. Since it was developed over time, it can also be revised over time. As we have seen, you can begin to do this by speaking out and acting out, which will immediately give you concrete evidence that your self-concept is faulty. In this third step, clearing out, you purposely construct a healthier self-concept by clearing away the old messages and creating new ones.

That's why the first part of your clearing out process should be to clear a space in your consciousness for a new self-concept to develop. You can kick off this process by developing awareness—noticing how much negativity there is in how you currently think about yourself. From now on, instead of indulging in these critical remarks, simply start saying to yourself that you're not going to listen to them anymore. It may seem strange to think that just telling yourself not to do something will work, but it will. In the same way you listened to all the negative things you said about yourself—and responded by building a negative self-concept—so, too, can you turn off these voices, let them float off into the ethers, and let a more self-affirming view of yourself emerge. When all this negative self-talk is out of the way, the real you will have a chance to show itself.

You can speed up the development of your positive self-concept by creating what I call *The Self-Concept Book*. Here's how you do it: Buy a little book that attracts you, and from now on, each time someone says something complimentary about you, write it in your book. For example, if, in a passing conversation, someone says that you're a wonderful listener, that you're so funny, or that you have a wonderful smile, write it down. It may seem pedestrian, but the more you do this, the more your internal messages will be changed. Instead of being cluttered with all the old messages about your inadequacies, your interior space will begin to fill with a positive awareness of who you are.

As you continue to write these things down, you'll also notice that all the people who observe you will tend to have a consistent response to who you are. A number of people will mention your beautiful smile, batches of people will notice how funny you are, most of the people you know will mention your sparkling intellect or your great taste in clothes. Instead of feeling like the battered, tattered, inadequate person you used to think you were, you'll realize that there are beautiful, amusing, precious, and extraordinary things about you. A new picture of who you are will emerge.

How to Support Your New Self-Concept

Along with creating your new positive identity, you will also need to support it by clearing away the people, experiences, and habits that reinforce the way you used to think of yourself. My friend T.J., who grew up in Harlem, left his entire family and went west because they kept telling him he was a loser and that one day he'd get killed by a street gang. Feeling so defeated by their opinion but somewhere inside believing better of himself, he got on a bus, and headed for California. For years his family had no idea where he was—they probably thought he'd been killed by a street gang. Once in California, he developed a serious meditation practice, discovered his spiritual side, and became a practicing Buddhist. Years later, when he learned that, ironically, his father had been murdered, he returned home. With his spiritual calm, he was the person who supported the other members of his family through this tragedy. He brought them tranquility and they in return, gave him a gift. They responded to him with praise and appreciation, an amazed but solid recognition of who he had become.

A happy ending isn't always the outcome when you clear out the people who don't support you. Sometimes your own positive development will go perpetually unnoticed. For example, after years of being ridiculed by her older brothers for being a bookworm and having a big head, Brette ran away from home, got a job at a K-Mart, and put herself through college and graduate school. Eventually she became an expert on children's learning disabilities and wrote a definitive book on the subject. A few years later, when she was invited by the university in her hometown to be part of their guest lecture series, she was surprised to notice her two brothers and several cousins in the audience. Her talk, a smashing success, was written up in the local paper, but none of her relatives so much as came out of the audience to acknowledge her. Although she felt hurt, rather than trying to make contact or seek their approval, she joined her university colleagues for a celebratory dinner and left town without making any contact with her family members. To this day, she hasn't spoken to them.

Clearing Out and Self-Love

Whether what you need to clear out is bad energy, old objects, bad attitudes, negative things you say about yourself, old habits, people who irritate you and run your life in a wrong direction, or whether you simply need to clear out some space to make room for new things to come in, it's terribly important to clear out what doesn't belong in your life. That's because whenever there's a space—in your living room, your psyche, your soul, your desk drawer, your closet, or your unconscious—that's occupied by something that doesn't serve you or affirm you, there isn't room for something that does—the new dress, the great idea, the man you can love, the belief in yourself. When a space is occupied, it's occupied. When your life is filled with junk, it isn't filled with joy; when it's filled with self-loathing, it certainly isn't filled with self-love.

It's a law of physics that nature abhors a vacuum. What this means is that nature seeks to fill emptiness with fullness. It's as if nature looks upon emptiness as an invitation, an opportunity to provide something. If a space is full, it's clearly filled. If it's empty, on the other hand, it's inviting nature to do some magic, to bring something in. This is exactly what nature—God, the force, or whatever you want to call it—does best. Like a good inn-keeper, Nature loves to fill up the vacancies, but if a space is already occupied, Nature assumes that everything's as it should be, and Nature moves on.

The laws of physics won't do battle with the status quo. And so the new thing, person, experience, attitude, friend, lover, outlook, habit, hat, pet snake or puppy won't fight and snarl to find its way in. It will only come in if there's already room. The vacancy is the invitation. The clearing is the come-on. The new whatever-it-is has a sense that you're wanting and waiting, happily anticipating. It wants to feel welcome; it wants to know that there's room. Out there, wherever it is, it's hoping you'll clear a space for it. It wants you to love yourself by inviting it in.

Why It's So Hard to Clear Things Out

It's very difficult to clear things out, even when you know you should. There are a couple of reasons for this. As souls, we come to life clear, a *tabula rasa*, as the ancients say. That is, we arrive in the world like a clear tablet of paper upon which nothing has been written. The expression tabula rasa actually means a tablet of stone upon which perhaps many things have already been written, but the stone has been ground down, razed, so that all the previous messages or information have been ground away by the motion of the grinding stone. Such a stone tablet was one of the earliest means of writing. That's what we're like when we arrive in the world. Even if you subscribe to the notion that each of us has multitudes of sequential past lives, when we arrive in this one, the tablet of our individual souls has been razed down to its whiteness. On this clear stone, the stories of our lives are written. Word by word, syllable by syllable, tragedy by tragedy the markings of our individual stories are inscribed on the tablet of our personalities and souls.

What I described earlier as our life themes are gradually imprinted on our psyches. From the pristine clarity of our consciousness at birth, the white stones of our souls become muddied and corrupted by the people, experiences, teachings, losses, confusions, violations, and abuses that are part and parcel of human existence. Instead of being able to respond to life from clarity, we experience confusion. Instead of knowing, we have questions. Instead of having confidence in the beautiful selves we are, we have discomfort, uncertainly, crises in self-esteem, niggling little self-doubts, and ugly doses of self-loathing.

Because we're all trying to fix whatever it is we're suffering from, we're also very attached to the ways we developed in order to try and fix the problem. Willem, for example, grew up in terrible poverty. In his homeland in Europe, he earned pennies a day leading a blind beggar around in the streets. In his family's house, basically a hut on the far corner of a farmer's field, there was neither plumbing nor heat. Will was the middle of eleven children. On weekends he went with his father to shovel peat from the peat bogs to stoke the fire in the fireplace. Obviously, his young life was marked by the terrible abuses of mere circumstance caused by his large family and his father's inability to provide. To compensate, Will went to work. Gradually, as he acquired a small means, he became entranced with the beautiful objects of life. When he came upon a book that intrigued him, or a beautiful vase or pair of shoes, he made sure he worked enough that he could acquire it. He was compensating for his wound.

As time went on Will worked so hard that he had the means to acquire many things. His life became an opera of acquisition. Soon he couldn't restrain himself. He wanted everything he saw. He was driven to working harder and harder in order to acquire more and more things. Finally, he was surrounded by things. Buried by his possessions. Overwhelmed. In time, he began to hate himself for surrounding himself with the chaos of all his possessions, but still he felt unable to rid himself of them. Even the thought was frightening. Getting rid of them was like getting rid of a part of himself. He was torn between his self-loathing for having created a life made insane by his vast collection of possessions and his fear of getting rid of any of them.

Like Will, we all have things—though of course they're not all actual possessions—that represent both the way we've tried to heal ourselves of the pain of our childhoods and also the way we've become less than fully loving of ourselves.

If you've wrapped your body in fat in order to protect yourself from the pain of your sexual abuse, you probably judge yourself for the extra weight you're carrying around. If you've become so brilliantly intelligent and argumentative because your father never honored your intelligence, you probably dislike it that you're so overbearing in relationships that you keep losing friends. If you've become an emotional accommodator because your mother overwhelmed you and the only way you could get her attention was to cater to her every whim, you probably hate yourself for being such a patsy. If you throw yourself at men because your father never acknowledged your beauty, you probably beat yourself up for making such a fool of yourself. If you take on responsibility for everyone else because your mother was a lunatic alcoholic who let the house run wild, you probably hate yourself for being an exhausted wreck because you try to keep everyone in line.

Whatever you've done to compensate for the pain in your childhood is probably the very thing you beat yourself up for now. It's also the thing you need to change, to clear out of your life.

Compensation and Attachment

What makes it so difficult to clear out whatever we need to clear out of our lives is that we become invested in the way things are. We like the behaviors we've developed to compensate for what happened in our childhoods. They're familiar. For a time, they were our only lifeline. They're how we survived. It's scary to think of giving them up. What will we do without them? What will we replace them with? By now, they're the way we define ourselves. Who would we be without them? We've become so attached that we can't imagine living without them.

We developed behaviors that were meant to help. We were trying to solve the problem of not being loved in the way we needed to be loved so we could grow up and lead our lives as the one unique self that we are. We coped—in hopes of having our spirits soar, but by now we're so bogged down by all these behaviors, that we're aghast and ashamed of them. They're not behaviors that are the true reflection of our souls. And they're certainly not the behaviors through which we're loving ourselves.

Whatever these are for you, whatever the coping mechanisms that you've developed, whether it's collecting a million objects, effacing yourself so much that you're only a shadow in any room you walk into, or serving everyone on the planet except yourself—you're very attached to it by now. Whatever you've done to try to fix the way you weren't loved well enough when you were a child has become, through your practice of it and your attachment to it, the way that you're not loving yourself right this very minute.

The Kinds of Clearing

There are a variety of clearings that you may need to do. Here are some of the most common:

Clearing Space

A lot of the clearing we need to do has to do with the literal spaces, structures, and circumstances in our lives, the personal geography of our existence. In these arenas, the focus is on clearing the material clutter. Sometimes it's as simple as clearing off your desk, weeding old clothes out of your closet, tidying up the cluttered garage. These are all forms of clearing out in the material world, and, as the Feng Shui artists tell us, this is a very important form of clearing. If your world is cluttered, your consciousness is cluttered also. Clearing out the spaces and structure of your life is a good place to begin. Like that opening in the forest, a clearing in the material structure of your world will create space for new objects and events to come in. It will also create a new sense of yourself. When you look at a world in tranquility, you yourself will feel more tranquil. When you look at a well-arranged closet, you will feel less chaotic. When there's space to breathe in, you will feel happier about being alive.

Like Will, Barb had a penchant for getting bogged down with stuff. Her parents had been very poor and as a child she was constantly told that she needed to hold on to things because "you never know when you might need it" or, "don't throw that away; you might never be able to get another one." Her parents saved paper bags and string, screws, nails, hinges, rubber bands, plastic bags, plastic food containers, and old clothes and shoes which they saved in bags in the attic. They taught Barb that she, too, should save everything; in fact, they punished her if they ever caught her trying to throw something away.

By the time she was an adult, Barb couldn't get rid of anything. Her apartment was cluttered with all the things she haphazardly acquired—old clothes, radios, and TV sets that people had given her, gifts and trinkets and cards people sent her, circulars that came in the mail, free samples of products she felt obligated to pick up at the health food store. Whatever anyone gave her, Barb kept, whether she needed it or not. As time went on, she felt that these things were more important than she, that taking care of them was her job. She was a prisoner of her stuff; she couldn't keep up with it all.

Not long after she showed up in therapy to talk about her problem, Barb decided to change jobs. A few weeks later, her colleagues at work threw a party for her. In appreciation for her time with them, they gave her a lot of cards and a whole lot of gifts and trinkets she didn't need and had nowhere to put in her apartment.

Barb learned that her over-involvement with things was the way she had compensated for the way her parents hadn't loved her. This time, instead of trying to find a place for all the stuff she'd been given at the party, Barb put it all in a bag, and without looking at it a second time, she dropped it off at the Salvation Army. She told me that this was one of the scariest things she'd ever done; in fact, she almost went back and asked them to give the bag back to her. By the time she got home, she felt scared and guilty because she'd "wasted so many things," but shortly thereafter she started feeling "free." For the first time in her life she felt as if she was more important than all her stuff.

From this initial step, she hired a helper to assist her in cleaning out her entire apartment. She threw sixty more bags of stuff away. From the things she decided to keep she noticed that she had a real interest in art, in her own creativity. A few months later she started taking painting classes, and now she has exhibited her work in several shows.

Clearing Your Consciousness

> Awareness without judgment creates change.
> —Tim Gallwey

Even more important than clearing out your material world is the clearing of your consciousness, your personal awareness, the way you think about yourself and your life. These are subtle levels of clearing that provide room for internal growth and change. When you do this kind of clearing, you clean up the ideas and attitudes that clutter your unconscious, that have the capacity to torment you and keep you steeped in feelings of unworthiness. You also clear your conscious mind, the way you think and talk about yourself.

The first step to clearing your consciousness is to develop awareness. Maybe you haven't noticed how much you beat up on yourself, how you always seem to approach life from the position that nothing good will happen to you, that you're a loser. Perhaps you've never paid attention to the nasty words that play over and over in your mind. Until you notice what you're doing, you can't change it. Noticing is the beginning of change. What has your mind been saying to you, and how have you been responding? Do you agree with the self-damning voice, the one that says you're no good, you'll never make it, so why try anyway—or do you put up a fight and argue with that voice?

Clearing your consciousness is a conscious process. That is, you need to mindfully attend to it. You won't feel clear simply because you decide you'd like to feel better about yourself, or you wish you weren't so hard on yourself. Sometimes the process of developing your awareness and shutting out the things that aren't healthy and helpful for your consciousness can be assisted by a therapist, spiritual teacher, or witness. An outside listener or watcher can often see you more clearly than you can see yourself. He or she can help you identify the unkind words, attitudes, feelings, and habits you need to clear out.

Mara had a million ways of verbally beating up on herself. When she got up in the morning she'd look in the mirror and say, "Oh, my God," as if she'd just encountered a witch. When she looked in her closet to dress, she'd bawl herself out for not having anything decent to wear. When she got to work, she'd beat herself up because her desk was a mess, she wasn't accomplishing enough. She wondered why her boss had hired her anyway—she wasn't smart enough for the job. The litany continued when she got home. She didn't know what to fix for dinner and she criticized herself for not planning meals better. This went on until she went to bed—when she condemned herself for staying up so late.

The nagging self-loathing voices were always the harshest when Mara would lie awake in the middle of the night. Then she would really go at it—recounting all her stupidities and limitations, until she was beaten to shreds emotionally.

When she told me about her relentless voices, and we talked about her past, it was apparent that her inner voices were the reruns of her parents' non-stop stream of brutalizing commentary, judgment, and criticism: "Why are you so stupid; why can't you ever do anything right? Who'd ever pick you for anything? Where on earth did you get that outfit? Who'd want you for a friend? You look like a corpse, wearing all that makeup." As Mara repeated this ream of emotionally devastating remarks, she fell apart in my office. These vicious comments were so deeply embedded in her psyche that for her entire life she'd done nothing but repeat them to herself.

I suggested that since she already knew how to talk to herself, she could change the content of what she was saying—keep talking, but say something different. The first thing I suggested was that when she woke up in the night and the voices started taking her apart she should quietly and firmly say: "I'm not going to listen to that anymore." It was simple, and she did it. She reported that it worked immediately. The negative, self-loathing voices went away.

Then I encouraged her to make a list of what she needed to say to herself to displace the violent voices. Here's what she wrote:

- I will only speak to myself with love, confidence, and respect.
- I will only listen to people who reflect the best about me.

Living by these two rules has been a challenging journey for Mara; but the more she repeats them to herself, the more she values herself, and the more she is able to receive the praise that others express.

To support herself in this process, Mara also used a simple behavior modification tool—buying a circlet of wooden prayer beads she wore on her wrist. She would touch the beads and say a sentence of self-praise after she made an unkind comment about herself. This method may seem simplistic, but it is a very powerful ways of regrooving mental attitudes. It worked for Mara. It could work for you.

Clearing the "Vibes"

Another form of clearing is energetic clearing. In this kind of clearing you get rid of energies that have the power to drain you. On a subtle level, rather than supporting you in the path of loving yourself, certain energies affect your ability to stand strong for yourself and proceed down your path with confidence. There are several kinds of energetic clearings. Sometimes you must clean out the energy of a person, sometimes of a place. Many people I know engage a shaman or healer to "clear" a new house when they're moving into it. What they're asking for, really, is that the energies of the people who lived there before will be removed, making space for the feelings, objects, and events that will arrive with the new owners. Most of us don't feel the subtle energies that reside in a house. We'll walk into a house, like the colors, the number of rooms, or the yard and say, "This is it, we like it, let's buy it."

But just as our emotional histories lay down an imprint on the very skins of our cells, so too the energies of people who have occupied the houses and spaces we come to leave a mist, an imprint of their energy. When we enter a place they've occupied, we're also entering the energetic input that they left there. This is true not only of physical spaces, but also of our bodies, where our emotional and physical connections to others leave traces of their energy. It's not that all these mists or traces are negative or necessarily bad; it's just that they're there. They leave a film which sometimes makes it difficult to see what we need to see, or be what we are trying to be in that particular situation or environment.

Once when I was visiting New York, I was graciously offered the apartment of a friend so I could work on the book I was writing at the time. My friend had just moved into the apartment and then had gone on vacation leaving a key for me under the doormat. It was a lovely sunny afternoon when I arrived. There was a beautiful desk in the living room and I set out all my writing things. As I looked out the window the view of the river was beautiful. Above it the sky was streaked with white clouds. Yet when I sat down to write I felt a strange discomfort. I got up, wandered around some, got myself a drink of water, and sat down once again. This restless roving continued for hours. Finally, although I didn't know why, I felt I could never be comfortable there, either to write or to sleep. I packed up my things, called a cab, and went downtown to a hotel.

Weeks later when my friend return from her holiday she asked me how I'd liked her apartment. Expressing my appreciation, I had to tell her that, actually, I'd never been able to use it. I told her about my strange discomfort and how I'd finally left. She listened with curiosity, and we finished our conversation. Weeks later we spoke again on the phone and she told me that, in talking with her neighbors, she'd learned that shortly before she moved in, a man who was dying of cancer had lived in the apartment, and during his final anguishing days, he'd shot himself to death. Traces of his energy were what, apparently, I'd felt. Not long after, my friend had the apartment cleared with sage and herbs by a Native American medicine woman; but six months later, she moved out because she, too, was never able to feel entirely comfortable there.

For both my friend and me, this apartment contained an energy that would not have served us well if we had stayed in its presence. Loving ourselves meant, in my case, leaving the afternoon I arrived, and in her case, leaving some months later. Although such actions might seem absurd to some people, the effect of the remaining energies of suicide were noticeable to both of us; removing ourselves from them constituted an act of self-love.

Sometimes the energies you have to clear will be attached to an object or objects you possess. For example, Crystal had a set of luggage that her boyfriend bought for her. It was beautiful and, she knew, very expensive. When he gave it to her, she was impressed that he'd given her such an extravagant present. Crystal traveled a lot, and so the luggage was a thoughtful gift. However, even at the beginning, she noticed the suitcases were very heavy—heavier, she felt, than she'd be able to comfortably handle. After accepting the luggage and thanking her boyfriend profusely, she mentioned her concern about the weight to him in a very delicate way. Rather than responding with care or concern, her boyfriend told her he'd done a lot of research and this was by far the best luggage all around. He assured her that in time she'd get used to the weight.

For several years Crystal traveled with this luggage. Because of her boyfriend's sales pitch, she thought she'd get used to the heavy bags, but they were always hard for her to manage. Often when she came back from a trip, she'd feel so achy she'd have to schedule a massage, and the masseur who worked on her would teasingly say he could feel a suitcase in each of her shoulders.

In time Crystal and her boyfriend broke up. Once, when she was traveling she saw some inexpensive lightweight silver luggage. She looked at it longingly, but since the luggage her boyfriend had given her was still very solid and strong (and he had predicted it would be) she didn't buy the new luggage. The following year when she returned to the same town on a business trip, she once again saw the silver luggage in a department store. This time she bought it. She brought it home and put it up in her closet, and it delighted her eye. She wanted to throw the old luggage away, but somehow she just couldn't make herself do it. Her closet was crowded, but each time she thought of throwing her boyfriend's luggage away, his words would haunt her.

Then she noticed that there were some things about the design of her new luggage that weren't as practical as the luggage her boyfriend had bought her. Beating herself up for making a mistake, she decided to use her boyfriend's heavy luggage for a trip she was about to take. As she was packing, she suddenly remembered how her father had always made her carry heavy boxes of nails and huge pieces of lumber when he was working on a project. Her father, a contractor, had wanted her to be a boy, so she could be a partner in his business. He had treated her like a boy and had never allowed her to have anything pretty.

When Crystal made this connection, she started to weep. She saw how in submitting to her boyfriend's demands about the luggage, she had experienced once again her father's hard treatment of her. In a fit of rage she went to the closet, took down the luggage, drove it out to the county dump, and watched with glee as it got mashed. As she drove away, she felt as if she was finally loving the girl her father had never accepted. She started using the silver luggage, and to this day cites her purchase of it as the moment she started the journey toward loving herself.

Like Crystal, you may find yourself snagged by some weirdly troublesome object or experience. Look for its connection to your past and clear out whatever you need to in order to start loving yourself.

"Firing" People

On an energetic level, we are always bathed in the aura and the energy of the people with whom we have interactions. The more we're aware of ourselves, the more we're also aware of how other people's energies affect us. For example, you may notice that you don't really have fun every time you go shopping with your friend Mary. Somehow instead of enjoying the frolic of shopping, Mary's always talking about how there's nothing nice in the stores anymore, how everybody who's walking down the sidewalk doesn't know how to dress, and how the coffee you just got at the charming Viennese coffee bar really wasn't very good. Rather than having fun on your shopping jaunt, you now feel drained and depressed, and, funny, you've noticed over the years that everything you've ever bought on a shopping trip with Mary you've ended up not liking very much. In fact, the purchases you've made while shopping with her always end up in your throw-away bag. Mary's someone you'd do well to fire from your life. She doesn't lift—she drains—your energy.

The same is true of lots of other people in our lives. Some of them are "drainers" like Mary. Some of them are "users," people who always need and take without ever returning the favor. Some have simply fulfilled their purpose in your life, and now it's correct that you move on from them.

Corporations and businesses fire people who don't do their jobs well, who aren't serving the purpose of the company, or who are misplaced in their jobs. You can—and should—fire the people who no longer belong in your life.

Elaine had a friend named Lynn whom she had met shortly after she moved to a new neighborhood. One night Elaine became very ill, collapsed on her living room floor, and called out for help. She was responded to by a neighbor whom she had never met before. Walking by with her dog, Lynn had heard Elaine's cries and came to her rescue. She called an ambulance and got Elaine to the hospital, where it was discovered that she was in anaphylactic shock, having suffered a severe allergic reaction to shrimp.

As a result of this "rescue," Lynn and Elaine became friends, started going to movies together, and occasionally out to dinner. Early on Elaine began to notice that she didn't really feel comfortable with Lynn, but because of her gratitude at Lynn's having virtually saved her life, she persisted in sharing social occasions with Lynn and treating her like a friend.

After some time, Lynn started dropping by Elaine's house, planting herself on the sofa, turning on the TV, making herself at home, and initiating mindless conversations. Since Elaine had a demanding day-job and was also a nighttime student of massage, Lynn's interruptions were difficult. From time to time Elaine would tell Lynn that she'd really prefer it if Lynn didn't show up without calling first.

Time went on and Lynn ignored these requests and kept showing up uninvited. She also continued to want to do things with Elaine. Since most of these things seemed innocuous, Elaine continued to do them, but she never particularly enjoyed them. One night she mentioned to Lynn that she was looking forward to finishing her massage class and getting a job on a cruise ship. When she said this Lynn launched into a long diatribe about what an impractical life this would be, how crazy Elaine was to consider doing it—it wasn't a reliable income—and besides people could take advantage of you while you were out there on the ocean sailing around in a boat. Especially if you were giving massages.

The night this happened, Elaine reached her limit. She finished the evening and the next day called Lynn and left a message saying that their friendship no longer served her, and that she needed to end it. Lynn left her own message telling Elaine that she was the most selfish person she had ever known—how could she do this after Lynn had saved her life? She then suggested that Elaine was just tired and that she'd better call back and apologize so the two of them could go to a movie on Friday night. Rather than responding to this emotional abuse, Elaine simply disregarded the message, wrote Lynn a note reiterating her original statement, and quietly went on with her life.

As Elaine went through this process, she remembered that when she was a little girl her grandmother had tended her after she'd almost died of encephalitis. Later, when her grandmother was old, she came to live at Elaine's parents' house. By then Elaine was a teenager and although her grandmother had become very crotchety and demanding, Elaine waited on her hand and foot, until finally her grandmother died. It never occurred to her to refuse anything that her grandmother asked because she had taken such good care of Elaine when she was a little girl.

As Elaine went through the process of liberating herself from her "friend," she realized that she had been susceptible to Lynn's bad treatment because of her experience with her grandmother. She realized that she'd also had several other relationships like this, and that she'd always felt unworthy of asking for better treatment because she "felt indebted to them somehow." From then on Elaine decided she would only allow a person into her life if she had chosen that person, and that giving herself the power to choose was a way of loving herself.

Clearing Your Body

Your body is the receiver of all the psychological and physical messages that have ever been imprinted on it. Chiropractors treating adults can find evidence of infant trauma in the skulls and spines of their patients. You may fall from a highchair when you're eight months old. Your mother may grab you and once you've stopped crying, assume that you're all right. She's right. Nothing life threatening has happened, but just the same, the impact of that trauma has been recorded in your skeleton. It's the same with all the psychological events we experience, the drugs we take, food we eat, sounds we hear, images we see, gestures of affection we receive. All these, too, will express themselves through your body, in your health, in your physical appearance, in the amount of weight you carry, your physical stamina, and how you feel, emotionally, about the amazing temple of your spirit.

Numerous common physical ailments have a direct relationship to the foods we eat. Depression has been linked to sugar and alcohol. ADD has been linked to red and other colored food dyes. That doesn't mean that all depressions or all ADD is food-related, but it does mean that what we ingest, what we take into our bodies in any number of other ways, can significantly affect our behavior and the way we feel about ourselves.

We live in a toxic world. There are hundreds of chemicals that are clearly identified by the United States Food and Drug Administration as toxic to the delicate human organism. We ingest, inhale, wash our hair, or paint our fingernails with poisons every day. We are surrounded by toxic substances at work and in our home environments in the form of paint, synthetic fabrics, and carpets. All these affect our physical health and emotional outlook. These chemicals create disease, shorten our lifespan, and impinge on how we feel about ourselves. The person who lives in a radiantly healthy body generally feels far better about himself or herself than the person whose body is a toxic waste dump.

As with all other forms of clearing, the first step in clearing your body is awareness. You need to educate yourself about all the substances to which your body is routinely exposed, and then decide which steps you are willing to take. Or you'll have to evaluate the meaning of the extra weight you carry, and adopt a program to help you with it. There are many avenues for physical clearing—fasting, dietary changes, weight loss plans, and twelve-step programs among them.

Mike had smoked dope for years—ever since he was in college. He didn't smoke himself into a stupor, but he did smoke every day. Even more than physically, he was psychologically addicted. He realized that each day when he came home from work he could think of nothing better to do than to sit on the couch and get stoned.

Mike was a successful young architect and, although he rationalized it in quite a few ways—I'm still young, my job's really stressful, I wouldn't do it if I had a girlfriend, everybody deserves to relax—he really hated himself for having this habit. Instead of being able to value himself for his successful career, he beat up on himself because all he could do every night was come home and get stoned. Now, along with getting stoned every night, he was telling himself what a rotten person he was *for* getting stoned every night.

One night he realized that no matter what he had achieved as a child, his father had always found a way to criticize him for something he hadn't done right. He'd get all A's on his report card, for example, but his father would criticize him for not putting the lawnmower away just right in the family garage. He'd win the basketball trophy, and his father would put him down for getting a B in science.

Mike finally realized that he was treating himself just the way his father had treated him. He had developed a bad habit—for which he was criticizing himself—and was overlooking his really quite substantial achievements. Perhaps, it occurred to him, he had developed the habit precisely so he could treat himself the way his father had treated him, because this treatment was so familiar! The night he had this realization, Mike stopped smoking dope, and in sixteen years has never taken it up again. When he speaks of this experience he tells of how he wept for many days after he quit smoking. "I'm sure it was the chemical withdrawal," he said, "but on a deeper level I know it was because I was finally loving the kid my father had never loved, accepting myself as I am."

The Joy of Clearing

Like the people referred to in this chapter, as you discover the areas you need to clear out, you will find to your great delight and amazement that wonderful things begin to happen. The universe will step in to support you. It will bring you gifts—new people and experiences, space, and opportunity, and above all, a cherishing sense of yourself. Less is more. Emptiness fills. The new will make the old irrelevant.

So take a moment now to think about this question: as far as you know, in what areas do you need to do some clearing out? Go over the kinds of clearing you need to do and make a commitment to start clearing in at least one of these arenas this week.

EIGHT

Set Out

*You can never solve the problem at the level of the
problem...*

—Maharishi Mahesh Yogi

There is really only one way to arrive at authentic self-
love, and that is to realize that you can never be fully
satisfied on a psychological level. The "terrible errors of
childhood" as the poet William Stafford once called our
psychological wounds, can never be entirely redressed in a
single human lifetime. Although you can take many steps
toward claiming yourself on a psychological level, the true
reception of the miracle you are can only be perceived in
a higher frame.

When you're stuck in a traffic jam—tires squealing, horns banging, people yelling at each other—the hostility of the whole world seems to be concentrated on a single street corner, and the world feels like an angry place. At other times you can be in an airplane and see the vast and beautiful expanse of the planet, where cars are ants, huge office buildings mere pinpoints of light, and the earth seems like a tranquil and beautiful place.

It's the same with loving ourselves. The picture always has two frames. On an emotional level, learning to love yourself is an undertaking of the personality. It means that, just as you are, a person stumbling, bumbling, and celebrating your way through life, you desire the tranquility of feeling good enough to proceed, finding peace in your heart when you sleep at night, having confidence as you move through the vicissitudes of your life. But on a higher, spiritual level loving yourself is loving your essence, and that is quite another matter.

If you have applied the teachings of the first three steps in this book, you've probably already found a greater sense of comfort in your life, as well as real moments of loving yourself. True self-love, however, the unshakable joy of recognizing the you I spoke of at the beginning of this book can never be attained simply by shoring up your broken-down psyche. In addition to the first three steps, which deal on the psychological level, you must somehow come to an awareness of a higher self, the you beyond the you, the self beyond your personal self, the eternal essence that stepped into life in the form of this you for a time.

This essence is beyond all the psychological dramas and traumas you have endured. It is beyond your heartaches and woes, beyond your achievements, and even beyond the legacy you'll leave behind. This you is nameless, faceless, radiant, and eternal. This you knows who you are and what you're doing here. This you understands that the whole wonderful, self-doubting, nerve-wracking trip of a single human life is all about love, is really only a teaching about the mystery and the majesty of the all-encompassing ocean of love that we have come from and to which we will return.

We are love, and everything we suffer and endure, go through or dream of is here to remind us of that single final fact. It's very hard to remember this. And because we can only occasionally remember this, because for a lot of us this concept is like some wild jungle animal roaming around in the vine-draped outskirts of our consciousness, we're usually trapped at the level of the relationship break-up, the traffic jam, the lost job, or the mother-in-law—stuck in our own little personal grade B movies with no concept whatsoever of the grand eternal Roxy Theater where all our little personal movies are playing—each one of them just a scene in the all time longest playing movie in the world; the one called love.

It's very hard to remember this.

Human life is simultaneously a path toward and a huge distraction from the grand and eternal truth that our lives are all about love. Indeed, the only way that we can really ever love ourselves is to somehow get in touch with this picture, to see that we're a part of the whole, to remember that we are love—and that we are loved.

To arrive at true self-compassion, you must see yourself as part of this whole, as deserving of belonging. In the eternal context, you do have a place, you are a being of infinite value, you have been chosen. Knowing this can bring great peace. But to arrive at this peace requires attention, a conscious turning. To arrive at a destination, you must set out.

You must set out on a new path, to a higher level, to what has greater meaning. You must move on from what you've always done, and set out in the direction of something new. In order to set out, you must begin by acknowledging that there's someplace beyond where you are that's worth going to, that you don't know it all, that you haven't arrived, and that there's more to receive.

Setting out implies an unknown—you take the first step, but you can't see your destination. There's a distance between you and it. You don't know what you'll find on the way—whether there will be disappointments or revelations, sidetracks and detours, dangers or miracles, tigers or angels. Nevertheless you set out—with the sense that something more awaits you, with the commitment to discover what that is. And the deeper you go with this commitment, the more of yourself you will find.

Sometimes we feel that the more we focus on ourselves, the better we'll love ourselves, and when you're dealing with your psychological issues, this is certainly true. Engaging in a process of emotional healing can take a great deal of time and focus, and, as we have seen, it's very important to become aware of your psychological issues. It's also important to find your voice and speak out, to take action, to clear away what stands in your way, to create inner and outer space for yourself. But after you've done all that, it's even more important to set out on a path of surrendering yourself to something that can show you that you are a part of the whole—not the whole of yourself, but the whole of the universe.

It is only in that context that the petty horrors of your life will finally dissolve, that the truest beauty of your self will finally emerge. This process of discovery is beyond the psychological. It is a spiritual journey. When you set out on this path, you will find your true essence.

Which Path Should You Take?

In a way it doesn't really matter which path you set out on. Any path, deeply committed to and followed with intention, can lead you to your deepest essence. In one of his stories, the writer Andre Dubus speaks of people who have practiced the spiritual path of Alcoholics Anonymous for many years. "You know that look they have," he says, "when they've been dry for years. Like there's a part of them that nothing in the world can touch." He's referring to that deep quality of self that is achieved when one has truly set out on a path. Similarly, when you're in an ashram in India, and you spend a day in deep meditation with thousands of others who are also meditating, you recognize among them the utterly beautiful and tranquil eyes of certain people who, clearly, have been meditating for years. It's obvious that these souls have moved beyond self-loathing, that they've surrendered to a larger purpose. It makes sense that they're not lying awake at night still trying to patch together the tattered quilts of their broken self-confidence. In some profound sense they love themselves; in the heart of their being, they know they're all right.

The same is true for you. When you set out on a path toward something higher, you will discover yourself. Not your personal self, but your holy beautiful self, the one whom you can't help but love. The *you* who can step out of yourself and give. That *you* will find joy in fulfilling your purpose. That *you* is willing to serve. That *you* can do nothing but love.

There are many paths that can take you to this deeper self. Physical disciplines, spiritual practices, skills developed to such a high level they take you out of yourself. There's a beautiful Korean physical and spiritual discipline called Dahn Hak which I have practiced for several years. It specifically instructs you to honor your body and yourself by, for example, touching your face and saying the words, "I love you, my beautiful face" or by putting your hand on your chest and saying, "I love you, my wonderful heart." It also provides the physical discipline by which these words become true on an energetic level in your body.

Any form of dance can also do this, whether a Sufi dervish, an Argentine tango, a flowing fox trot, or a sensuous samba. When you dance you connect with your own transcendence. Meditating can also take you to this deep place in yourself. Swimming will do it. Surfing will do it. Walking miles with your dog can do it. But it isn't just one dance that will do it, a single night at an AA meeting, one morning of Dahn Hak practice, or an hour of meditation every other week or so. When you set out on a path you must walk it—with grace, with commitment, with steadfastness. For only if you set out on it again and again will it truly support you. Only if you walk it will it give you ... you.

Each time you deepen the journey of the path you have set out on, you deepen your relationship with yourself. That's because the deeper you go, the more obstructions to your true nature will fall away. The more the obstructions to your true nature fall away, the more you will see your true essence. The more you see your true essence the more you will see that your true essence is love. The more you see that your essence is love, the more you will love and receive yourself. And the more you receive yourself, the less you will struggle with questions of self-love. This is the circle you start to draw the minute you set out on your path.

Kelly and Robert stumbled onto their path. Kelly, a graphic artist, and Rob, a software designer, were married and lived in an upscale apartment in New York. They were very successful and all their friends admired their dramatic apartment, their plethora of techno toys and their, in general, high-profile lifestyle. But Rob and Kelly weren't happy. They often picked on each other, because, inside, neither one of them felt like a success.

Kelly often told Rob that if only she were a better graphic artist, she'd have a bigger salary and more of the things a successful person had. Rob told her she shouldn't feel so bad; he was a man, he felt even worse—although he was pretty successful, there were thousands of guys way more successful than he.

Kelly and Rob went around and around in these circles week after week. One night when Kelly came home, she started watching TV while she was making dinner. She'd often done this before, but she was a little depressed on this particular night. A colleague in her graphics firm had just landed the juicy contract she herself had hoped for. She watched the news, which was all about war and bombings, and then the half dozen commercials that said her hair wasn't shiny enough, she didn't have the greatest car, and she was using all the wrong cleaning products. Kelly started getting even more depressed, feeling really lousy and worthless. As she tells it, just then, something snapped. She turned off the TV, walked into the living room, sat down, and turned off all the lights.

When Rob came home and asked her what she was doing, she said she didn't know. She said she thought she was resting, but she wasn't sure. Instead of turning on the lights, Rob sat down beside her. He, too, was depressed. On the subway he'd been reading the paper. More news of war and corporate dishonesty. He'd suffered more losses and felt like a failure. In the dark, he started talking to her. He told her how empty he felt, how he was losing the rat race, how he looked at others and saw them succeeding in the fast-paced competitive world. He was falling behind by the day, by the minute. He wanted something different— he didn't know what. Kelly listened, then responded, saying she felt the same. There must be a new path, they both felt, but they didn't know what it was.

Following this, Kelly and Rob began to change many things. They stopped watching TV and they cancelled the paper. Kelly started doing yoga. Rob learned a meditation technique. Eventually they shared what they had learned with each other. They grew closer. Felt more centered. More self-accepting. And ultimately more generous.

When they looked at their pasts, Rob and Kelly both realized that they had each been the favored child in their family; in fact, they were both a little spoiled. Attached to this special status, however, was also the unstated demand that they both be exceptional—get the best grades, go to the best college, get the best job, have the highest salary, marry the sexiest girl, the most successful guy.

They'd done all this and still felt empty inside. In choosing to take a stand, as Kelly put it, "to feed our souls," they started to love themselves for the first time. Despite continuing ruffles in their respective professional lives, Rob and Kelly found inner peace, a greater sense of connection with one another, and a deep sense of gratitude for life.

Eventually, they adopted a little girl from China. Watching her grow, they decided to move from the city. They bought a farm where they each set up a consulting business, and started a tuition-free summer camp for underprivileged children. They have found meaning in their lives through inner quiet and outer service.

The Nature of Your Path

If you don't feel comfortable in a place, offer your work and you will see that immediately you are a part of it.

—Gurumayi Chidvilasananda

In an old fable about the creation of the world, it is said that there's an angel who whispers a message to each soul who comes to earth, a message of instruction about what each soul is supposed to do here when it arrives. Although many people wondered what complicated instructions the angel might have been giving each soul, the angel's message was simple. It consisted of a single word: *give.*

Sometimes we think the path we should set out on is the one through which we will finally transcend our fears, get rid of our self-loathing, and then just relax for the rest of our lives. That sounds enticing, but the truth is that some of the deepest paths to loving ourselves are those in which we serve others. Indeed, there is no easier—or more profound—way for you to discover how valuable you are, how meaningful your life is, how much you have to offer, what a beautiful heart and soul you have—than to set out on a path of service.

And whosoever would lose his life shall find it.

—Jesus Christ

After two divorces, Carrie, in her mid-forties, was shocked to realize that she was really a very self-centered person. Her first husband complained that "all she ever thought of was herself," and divorced her because she was so totally unsupportive when he got laid off from his job. Her second husband divorced her because she was so self-involved that she refused to have any relationship whatsoever with his two children from a prior marriage. After this second divorce Carrie was so devastated at being left a second time that she determined to discover what it was about her that had caused her to be rejected once again.

Through her personal growth work, Carrie realized that both of her husbands had been right—she was a completely self-obsessed person. She also discovered, to her amazement, that her self-obsession was not a consequence of feeling so worthy that she deserved all this attention. Quite the opposite, she'd always felt that nobody loved her. Unconsciously she felt that only by endlessly fussing over and talking about herself was there any chance that she could finally "get good enough" to have somebody love her. Rather than being the fruits of healthy self-love, her self-obsession was, paradoxically, the way she acted out her feelings that she was utterly unworthy of love.

She saw that her narcissistic self-focus, as well as her inability to give to others, was a holdover from the desperation of her childhood, where she had been abandoned by her father, sexually abused by an older brother, and unprotected by her alcoholic mother.

Seeing the role alcoholism had played in her psychological development and seeking support for her growth, she enrolled in a twelve-step program. There she embarked on a path of living by the spiritual principles which have filled her life with a sense of well-being and worthiness. Instead of sitting around and worrying about her acrylic nails the way she used to, she now volunteers for hospice. She says she feels privileged to sit with the dying, to see the equanimity with which, so often, they prepare to leave the world, the gratitude they express for her simple acts of kindness.

She also says that for the first time in her life she really knows what it is to love herself. Through her capacity to give she has discovered a sense of her own worthiness. She has learned this, she says, by taking the attention off herself and giving to others, by finally seeing that from what she always considered to be her impoverished self, she has a wealth of love to give.

Like Carrie, Jack was looking outside himself for the solution to his "love problem," as he called it. He was frustrated because he could never seem to find a relationship.

All the women he went after just didn't have enough of the attributes he had carefully listed as necessary in any woman he might pick to be his partner. Jack was a successful computer troubleshooter and had a great deal of success in his work, so his failure to unearth a woman who matched up to his perfectionistic standards was very upsetting.

One day, as he was once again complaining about the mediocre women of the world, I suggested he stop looking for what he could get from a partner, and focus on what he might give. He was stunned when I said this. It had never occurred to him that a relationship was an exchange, an opportunity to give as well as receive love, and that instead of seeking "the perfect mate" he should consider what he might have to contribute to the person he loved. When he contemplated this, he broke down, realizing that, in his own opinion, he was emotionally and spiritually bankrupt, that he had looked toward "the perfect woman" to provide him with something that he himself did not possess.

After this epiphany, he decided that from now on, each time he met a woman, no matter what the circumstances, he would inquire about her. As he spoke with women, he was shocked to discover how many of them had been raped, how many were raising children alone, had been physically abused, had grown up in a household with an alcoholic parent, or had put themselves through school in order to become providers. Stunned by these revelations, Jack's heart cracked open. Suddenly he felt a calling to support and protect women. He educated himself in women's issues and became instrumental in opening a battered women's shelter. Eventually he married a woman who had none of the attributes on his original laundry list. He chose her because, like him, she was committed to the cause of supporting women.

Unlike Jack, who was waiting for it all to come to him, perhaps your reason for not giving is that you feel you don't have any talents, nothing significant to contribute. You're not a rock star or a doctor, not the originator of a dot-com; you haven't written a novel, built a hospital, started a fad, or created some original software. But there are thousands of opportunities for you to discover the talents of your heart, to discover what is yours to give. It doesn't have to be fancy. It could be as simple as putting one foot in front of the other.

There was a woman whose real name we forget but whom many of us remember as Peace Pilgrim. At a certain time in her life, she realized that the only thing that mattered to her was world peace. She gave away all her worldly possessions, bought a pair of tennis shoes and a sweatshirt, and started walking across the continent. Peace Pilgrim, it said in big white letters on her shirt. People saw her walking and asked her why she was walking. "For peace," she said. They wondered where her home was and she explained that she didn't have one. When they saw her message, they offered their homes so she could spend the night. Peace Pilgrim embodied the message of peace. Walking for peace was her life's work. She did it until she died.

Your Life Purpose

The more I give to thee, the more I have, for both are infinite.
—Shakespeare

Service is always related to purpose. And like Peace Pilgrim, you too have a life purpose, a specific reason why you were brought here. Unlike Peace Pilgrim, however, you may not yet have awakened with a sense of your purpose emblazoned across your heart. Sometimes a life's purpose is visible early on, as in the case of a child prodigy who realizes at age seven that his destiny is to be a concert pianist. But more often, awareness of a life's purpose, like everything else about you, is something that gradually develops. To hasten your discovery of your purpose, here are some things to consider.

First of all, your life's purpose is already lying in wait inside you. It's like the oak tree, waiting all folded up inside the acorn. You can't see the oak tree right now, but given time and nurturing, an oak tree is inevitable. The same is true of your purpose. Most people think their purpose is something they've never dreamed of, that one day it'll just fall out of the sky and bang them over the head, but interestingly enough, like the oak in the acorn, it's already there. Even more interesting, rather than being something you've never dreamed of, something weirdly off your path, your purpose is very likely related to your "wound." What I mean by this is that it is somehow connected to the very things that were so painful in your life, the things that constituted your life theme—the things that have also made it so hard for you to love yourself.

My friend Lisa was emotionally abandoned by her corporate executive father and had a crazy mother who was always telling her children that their house was being taken over by aliens and they were all being poisoned by interstellar dust. As a young child, Lisa became so anxious because of all these pronouncements that she developed severe eczema. Her hands and arms were covered with weeping sores. When she scratched them, they bled, causing open wounds along her hands and arms.

As she grew up, Lisa felt very self-conscious about her skin. She felt as if no one would ever love her, because of her "alligator skin." She felt as if she needed to hide. For a long time she was so convinced she was a pariah that she developed agoraphobia and was unable even to leave her house. In this way she kept demonstrating to herself that she was unworthy of being loved.

As Lisa gradually identified her life theme—emotional abuse and abandonment—and uncovered the painful circumstances she had lived through; she began to feel compassion for the little girl who had been so terrorized and terrified that her nervous system reacted by creating eczema and her emotions by creating agoraphobia. She began to take care of her own skin and it responded to her loving touch. Instead of hating her skin, she began to treat it with special care. She also began to notice others who were suffering from similar conditions. In time she became an aesthetician, one who treats and cares for skin. She has now spent more than twenty years healing those who suffer from the same and other skin conditions. She also frequently volunteers to assist with the skin care of burn victims. She has turned her wound into a gift.

Your own gift, and your own life purpose, is related, just like Lisa's, to the painful path of your past. If you wonder what your purpose might be, ask yourself not what you could force yourself into doing, but what you can't keep yourself from doing.

What comes naturally to you? Bossing people around, listening, caring for the sick, designing houses, telling stories, burying your head in a book? If you look carefully, you'll probably notice that what you love to do is somehow related to your wound: your mother was a scatter-brain so instead of having a mother, you had to take charge of your little brothers and sisters; you could never get your father to listen—you know the pain of not being heard; your grandmother, the only person who really loved you, got sick and died at your house; your parents were always moving so you kept trying to design them a house they'd like enough so they'd settle down; your mother was an alcoholic, so you hid out in your room reading books. You'll also see that each of these adaptations to your wound could be translated into a beautiful expression of your talents—being a manager, a psychologist, a nurse, an architect, an author or an editor—and that, according to how you choose to apply them, they can also constitute a lifetime of sacred service.

If you wonder how to apply your talents at this highest level, ask yourself to which type or person, group, or community you find yourself drawn. Are you delighted by children? Attracted by older people? Crazy about animals? Passionate about the plight of the poor? Wherever you're naturally attracted, that's where your energy will most easily flow to help you offer your highest service.

And above all, ask yourself simply—what is my heart inviting me to do? We serve best where we have strong feelings. Is your passion to serve an inner city hospital—even though all your MBA colleagues think you're nuts?

To be an artist—even though you studied business? To be a dancer—although you studied law? To make a million dollars and give it all away—even though your father taught you that money is the root of all evil? Whatever your heart is saying, listen; wherever it leads you, follow.

Remember, what you give doesn't even have to be a huge thing. Volunteer at a Girls Club, sign up at a hospice, choose a particular beggar, or a particular corner where any number of beggars may situate themselves, and give a dollar every day. Write to your Congressperson, write to the President, protest the war, educate the public, be the highest, finest, kindest, most loving human being you can be in every single situation, every minute of your life. Adopt a highway. Save the whales. Save the ocean. Pick up the trash along the freeway—or on your block of "the hood." Read for the blind, sit with the dying, say a prayer, raise a flag, sing a song.

The world is filled with sorrows. There will never be enough shoulders to receive all the tears that will have to be shed; give your shoulders. People are hungry and starving and lonely and afraid. Give them your money and your food, give them your hands and your arms and your heart. Give them your time, lend them your ears, give them your blessing. When you do good things for others, you will experience your own goodness. When you give your love, your own heart will be filled with love. And if you ever wonder whether you're good enough to do it, give it, or share it—whatever it is—do it, give it, share it more. For whenever you give, you receive. Not in what you've given back in return—but yourself.

NINE

Living with Self-Compassion

One must endeavor to love oneself abundantly.

—Sharon Salzberg

I t is said by some that the ethers are filled with souls just waiting in line to be born, to be called to the dance, to be summoned to earth. Your soul got called. You were chosen. That's a compliment of the highest order. It's a compliment because God—or whatever you call him or her or it—decided that you deserved the trip, that you were worthy of the chance. If you were loved enough by the force of life to give you life, how can you not also love yourself? How can you not live with self-compassion?

Compassion is a great word that contains the word passion. Passion is deep feeling. When we live with passion we live ... as though our life depended on it. We follow the lead of our strongest feelings; we make deep commitments to things; we live, we give, we love. We find what makes our hearts sing, what causes our spirits to soar, and we devote ourselves to these things.

Compassion is living with that same intensity of feeling toward the sufferings of life. We usually think of it as an emotional stance we hold toward others. When we live compassionately, the sufferings of others don't escape us. We are mindful of them. We feel them as if they were our own. Instead of avoiding, turning our heads from the pain, anguish, and disappointment another soul is bearing, we step into the circle of their pain and respond to what they're going through. We "feel for" them. And out of this wealth of feeling, we also give to them.

Compassion for others often precedes or displaces compassion for ourselves. Perhaps because another's suffering is "in our face," it registers. So it is that the paraplegic in his rolling chair or the blind man with his dog may pull at our heartstrings and cause us to respond, with feeling, words, or action.

But even the accomplished spiritual seeker I mentioned in chapter 1 said that it was only when his teacher asked him about his compassion for himself that he encountered the limitations in his ability to love. As he noticed, we don't often extend the compassion we give to others to ourselves.

As we have seen, there are a number of reasons for this, but the greatest among them is that somehow we haven't yet come to feel that our own sufferings are worthy of the great love and kindness we naturally extend to others. Our own lives are so familiar to us that we can't seem to get outside them and look across at ourselves with the eyes of compassion. Instead we dismiss our own anguish, saying, "well, that was a long time ago," or "that's just the way it is," or "that's just the way I am." We've lived with ourselves so long that our sufferings are invisible to us. They're just the way things are.

I do many workshops where people do deep emotional work in the presence of others. I've often noticed that even after doing a piece of work so profoundly moving that all the other participants in the workshop have been weeping, that same person may later, at dinner, for example, when people are commiserating, brush it off once again by saying such things as, "Oh, well, my life wasn't nearly as bad as Janet's. Or Joe's. Or Barbara's." That can be factually true of course, but the point is that, even after experiencing the things in their lives that are so deserving of their own love, people often revert to the knee-jerk position that they don't really need it. It's hard to see ourselves with compassion. We've lived with our sorrows all our lives. They're so familiar that we can't see them.

For this reason, the path to self-compassion is always a process. And it is a twofold process because it consists not only of all the actual steps you have to take to get there, but also all the steps in consciousness you have to take to get there. You have to do all the things you have to do—speak out, act out, clear out, and set out, but you also have to keep holding the conviction that self-compassion is a destination you—both your personality and soul—really need to get to. It's a simultaneous journey of action and conviction. Just as the ruts of self-loathing were developed over time, year after year as you jabbed yourself with unloving remarks, wore yourself out with hundreds of little acts of physical neglect, betrayed your spirit with a series of abusive relationships, so the royal road to loving yourself, *le beau chemin*, is also constructed by many thousands of increments.

Ultimately, self-compassion is a series of choices, a moment by moment conscious turning away from that which will harm your spirit toward that which will nourish and sustain you. It is choosing, in any particular situation, and over and over again, whether you'll treat yourself well or beat yourself up, whether you'll deny yourself, or treat yourself as lovingly as you'd treat your child or your most precious friend. Self-compassion means looking at yourself with kindness, with a conscious awareness of your sufferings, and in time, with a deep appreciation for the way you have transformed them.

The Trek to Gaza Hot Springs

Last year I took a remarkable journey. In celebration of our many years of friendship, my friend Rebecca and I decided to go to Bhutan, a little kingdom nestled in the Himalayas, which is also sometimes called Shangri-la. In planning for the trip, I learned of the Gaza Hot Springs, sacred springs high in the mountains to which people trek to find physical rejuvenation and spiritual renewal. I told Rebecca that, more than anything, I wanted to hike to the hot springs—a five-hour trek, according to our travel agent's literature—and so we included it on our itinerary.

When we arrived in Bhutan, we were met by the two young men who were to be our guide and driver for our journey. After a day of sightseeing, we were left at our hotel and told that the following day after traveling to a campsite in the mountains, we would camp for the night and then set out on our trek the following morning.

After flying halfway across the world, we were tired and reluctant to start the trek so soon after our arrival. Nodding off to sleep that first night we decided that in the morning we'd tell our guide we weren't ready, that we'd like to postpone the trek or perhaps even cancel it altogether. The next morning when our guide arrived, I tried to tell him this, but even as I was saying it, I felt a great loss about not seeing the springs, especially since he told us that because of our complicated schedule, if we didn't set out today, we'd miss it altogether. So it was that, weary from jet lag and not enough sleep, we both conceded, and after driving more than four hours, we finally arrived at our base camp.

After a wonderful dinner made by our cook and eaten by candlelight in a tent, we were shown to two little tents pitched in mud on the bumpy ground at the side of the mountain. Wearing sweaters, long johns, fleece pants, fleece gloves, and fleece hats and holding on to little heat packets to keep our hands warm, we each had a fitful night's sleep on the muddy rock-studded ground. The following morning our guide and driver were ready to lead us on the trek. It was a beautiful morning. High sun shimmered across the majestic mountains, turning them emerald green. Though I was still exhausted I was also very excited to get to the hot springs, which, we had learned, were situated in a high valley at an elevation of 9,200 feet.

The path was narrow and still muddy from the summer monsoons, but the vistas and all the vegetation were gorgeous. I was glad we had come. It was still early and I was looking forward to mid-afternoon when we'd be soaking our troubles away in the hot springs. The path grew steeper. From time to time, it seemed to head almost vertically into the clouds. Now and then I would have to rest for a minute before going on.

The noon sun shone strong. It was getting hot. As we walked, we drank water from the camelback water storage we were carrying on our backs. Turn after hairpin turn we trudged on, from time to time pausing to wait as the lovely Bhutanese people, their horses weighed down on either side with bags of supplies, passed by on the trail alongside us, shepherding their goods toward home.

Finally, after walking five or six hours, we stopped at a wide green meadow where a chorten, a religious sculpture made of several classical square and round shapes fastened one on top of another in a certain order, had been beautifully constructed. The cook handed us boxes of sweet mango juice and then set about preparing our lunch. Across the field our horseman with the four horses carrying our supplies rested and chatted with our guides.

As we sat there, trekkers approached from the other direction. Rebecca paused to talk with them. "Hot springs"—vaguely I heard those words, then saw their heads wagging—in amazement? disbelief?—I couldn't tell. I sat resting on the lawn until our lunch was served, then ate the meal of chicken, vegetables, and rice at a leisurely pace, looking forward to relaxing in the hot springs in another hour or so.

After lunch we trekked on. Now I was tired. The mango juice, pure sugar, had gone to my head. Several times I needed to stop and rest a little before going on. Ahead of me I could see my friend and her guide making speed, storming ahead up around turns. Each time after resting, my guide and I pressed on. For hours. Passing school children, rice fields, beautiful painted Bhutanese houses, prayer flags blowing in the wind. I was concerned. It seemed that by now we should be there. Clearly, we'd been walking for more than six hours. The sun was dangling in the west. It was starting to get cool, and a little while later, when I looked up, the sun had vanished entirely. Grey clouds had gathered and now were filling the sky.

"Do you think it could rain?" I asked my guide; and he assured me it couldn't.

Four hours later, we were still walking. By then Rebecca and her guide were long out of sight. When I called out her name, there was no answer. It started to sprinkle. It started getting dark. It got dark. The rain came down harder. Rebecca and I had both packed rain gear and flashlights but they were in our duffel bags, which were now miles ahead on the horses. Then it started raining for real. Pouring. Strangely, I now felt stronger. The effects of the mango juice had subsided, the lunch had started to kick in. Soon it was pitch dark. We could hardly see our way. Stones rolled loose in the rain, tumbling over our shoes, blocking our path, rolling down the side of the mountain. Barely able to see the path, my guide and I stumbled on, with only the light of a half moon to guide us, reflected from time to time on silver gum and candy wrappers scattered like crumbs on our path.

At that time my guide confessed that he had never before led a trek to the hot springs. Although he had been there himself, that was many years before. He also told me that he'd instructed the horseman to hurry ahead and then come back for us—but there was no sign of the horseman. He'd disappeared in the night. We were somewhere in the Himalayas, a thousand miles—it seemed—away from anywhere, exhausted, and with no idea how far we were from our destination. I began to realize that the people my friend had spoken to before—the ones shaking their heads—had probably come from the hot springs and knew how far we still had to walk. In pitch dark, we pressed on. I had already twisted my ankle a dozen times and was concerned about not being able to continue on. But I kept on walking, kept taking steps, kept putting one foot after the other, kept getting up when I fell, kept holding the vision of the hot springs, kept on believing that somewhere—at the end of this trail, though I'd never been on it before, in the middle of these mountains, though I'd never seen them before—was the beautiful Gaza Hot Springs. I'd be so happy—it would be wonderful—when we got there.

Finally, twelve hours and twenty miles after we'd started, in pouring rain, we made it to Gaza Hot Springs. There in the upstairs room of an ancient wooden building, my friend, Rebecca, was waiting. When my guide and I walked into the room, she broke into tears. She'd waited alone in the dark for two hours while her own guide had run ahead to get help. When, finally, he returned, she was so tired and scared from waiting so long, she'd had to be carried the last few miles to the camp. She was sure that my guide and I had died in the storm or had fallen off the mountain. Wet and weary, mud caked but victorious, we all sat up together, telling each other our stories, and drinking hot cups of Indian tea that the cook had prepared.

The next day we soaked in the hot springs for hours while a gentle rain pattered against the roof of the building that housed it. In this sacred valley high in the Himalayas, white mist shrouded trees, and our pain fell away. We soaked and drank tea and ate cookies, had wonderful conversations and gave great thanks for our strength and perseverance. Our journey had been much farther and harder than either of us had imagined, but now it blessed us with the sweet fruits of our efforts.

Lost in the mountains, waiting alone in the dark for her guide to come back with a flashlight, my friend had learned equanimity. On my long dark arduous trek in the rain, I found the physical strength and endurance I never before believed I possessed.

Your Trek

Your journey to self-compassion is like my trek in the Himalayas. It begins with the dream of a destination—loving yourself—but before you set out there's likely to be some resistance. Like us, you may want to cancel out on the very thing you thought you wanted the most. But then, encouraged by some outside forces—an inner guide who won't let you give up—and because your soul really wants you to do this, you surrender.

And so you set out on the journey. And struggle with pitfalls and backward steps, with complications and detours. Like our trek to the hot springs, your journey to loving yourself is also a trek worth the taking. You'll know that when you arrive. You'll know that when, after all the pain and confusion and effort and courage, you can finally think of yourself and care for yourself and speak and act and dream on your own behalf. You'll know that when you can abide in the still strong whole beautiful sense of who you are, when you know in your heart that you fully deserve your own compassion.

A Prayer for Self-Compassion

> *Be patient toward all that is unsolved in your life.*
> *Learn to love the questions themselves, until some dis-*
> *tant day, without your knowing, you will have lived*
> *into the answers.*
>
> —Rainer Maria Rilke

As you've walked your way through each one of these steps, you have been learning to love yourself. Now, as a final confirmation, I suggest that you create a prayer for your path, words you can say in support of your journey.

Ordinarily when we pray, we're reaching *out there*—to a higher something or other, to the God, person, being, or It who has all the strength and all the answers. But since you're a part of the whole, this God, strength, power, and all these answers are also a part of you. For this reason, I urge you to make your prayer not to the God-out-there but to the you-in-here. Ask yourself to love and honor you.

When I was a child, my father used to say a beautiful prayer for me each year on my birthday. When I want to remember to love myself, I recall the beauty of his prayers and use them for inspiration. In the spirit of that loving care, I offer the following prayer for you:

Dear_____,

I ask you to hold me tenderly in your care,

To honor me and cherish me, to celebrate all my gifts and powers, to comfort me in the difficult hours, to fill my heart and enlarge my soul, to walk with me in the path of service, so I can fulfill my purpose on this earth.

May I know every day that I belong.

That I am loved.

That I am loving.

Amen

You can use this prayer or write your own as a simple reminder to sustain you on your path.

And Now, Love Yourself!

Love yourself in every direction. Love your amazing beautiful body. Love your wonderful intricate mind. Love your heart and all its exquisite emotions. Love your infinite eternal spirit.

Care for yourself every day, every minute. Hold yourself in the great loving care of your own good heart. Curl up in your body each night when you sleep, and wake up in the light of your beautiful soul each morning when you arise.

My deep prayer is that through these pages you will have learned to nurture, nourish, replenish, and fulfill the heart, body, mind, and soul of the one and only, unrepeatable, exquisite being that is *you*.

About the Author

Daphne Rose Kingma is a psychotherapist who has helped thousands of individuals and couples improve their relationships. She speaks and conducts workshops. She has written extensively on love and relationships. Her books include *Coming Apart; True Love: How to Make Your Relationships Sweeter, Deeper, and More Passionate; Weddings from the Heart,* and *The Ten Things to Do When Your Life Falls Apart: An Emotional and Spiritual Handbook.*

To Our Readers

Conari Press, an imprint of Red Wheel/Weiser, publishes books on topics ranging from spirituality, personal growth, and relationships to women's issues, parenting, and social issues. Our mission is to publish quality books that will make a difference in people's lives—how we feel about ourselves and how we relate to one another. We value integrity, compassion, and receptivity, both in the books we publish and in the way we do business.

Our readers are our most important resource, and we appreciate your input, suggestions, and ideas about what you would like to see published.

Visit our website *www.redwheelweiser.com* where you can learn about our upcoming books and free downloads, and be sure to go to *www.redwheelweiser.com/newsletter/* to sign up for newsletters and exclusive offers.

You can also contact us at *info@redwheelweiser.com*.

Conari Press
an imprint of Red Wheel/Weiser, LLC
665 Third Street, Suite 400
San Francisco, CA 94107